P9-DHQ-650

WITHDRAWN

DANVILLE PUBLIC LIBRARY
DANVILLE, INDIANA

The Real McCoy

The Real McCoy

Georgia Hole

DANVILLE PUBLIC LIBRARY
DANVILLE, INDIANA

OXFORD
UNIVERSITY PRESS

OXFORD
UNIVERSITY PRESS

Great Clarendon Street, Oxford OX2 6DP

Oxford University Press is a department of the University of Oxford.
It furthers the University's objective of excellence in research, scholarship,
and education by publishing worldwide in

Oxford New York

Auckland Cape Town Dar es Salaam Hong Kong Karachi
Kuala Lumpur Madrid Melbourne Mexico City Nairobi
New Delhi Shanghai Taipei Toronto

With offices in

Argentina Austria Brazil Chile Czech Republic France Greece
Guatemala Hungary Italy Japan Poland Portugal Singapore
South Korea Switzerland Thailand Turkey Ukraine Vietnam

Oxford is a registered trade mark of Oxford University Press
in the UK and in certain other countries

Published in the United States
by Oxford University Press Inc., New York

© Oxford University Press, 2005

All rights reserved. No part of this publication may be reproduced,
stored in a retrieval system, or transmitted, in any form or by any means,
without the prior permission in writing of Oxford University Press,
or as expressly permitted by law, or under terms agreed with the appropriate
reprographics rights organization. Enquiries concerning reproduction
outside the scope of the above should be sent to the Rights Department,
Oxford University Press, at the address above

You must not circulate this book in any other binding or cover
and you must impose this same condition on any acquirer

British Library Cataloguing in Publication Data

Data available

Library of Congress Cataloging in Publication Data

Data available

Typeset in Scala and Fineprint by Paul Saunders
Printed in Great Britain
by Clays Ltd, Bungay, Suffolk

ISBN 0–19–280611–4

ISBN 978–0–19–280611–6

10 9 8 7 6 5 4 3 2 1

Contents

103362

Introduction

L ook in almost any book or newspaper, or listen to almost any speech or radio or television programme, and imagine what you're reading or hearing would be like if it had no figures of speech: no metaphors, no colourful phrases, just dry-as-dust, dull-as-ditchwater literal meanings. Metaphorical expressions and allusions give life and vibrancy to languages all over the world and have done so for as long as anyone can remember. Language is constantly changing and evolving: new phrases are invented and taken up by other people, while others fall out of favour. The origin of some of these expressions is very clear, as with *dry as dust*, for example. However, many are very puzzling, even if you possess an encyclopedic knowledge of all human activity and history.

This is where *The Real McCoy* comes in. The book doesn't, of course, aim to tell the story of every phrase in the English language (a mammoth and virtually impossible task!). Instead it focuses on those phrases which are widely known and in current use today and which have a particularly interesting history, shedding light on obscure and surprising origins and sometimes dispelling a few myths and old wives' tales along the way. Some of the expressions are very ancient (such as *at sixes and sevens*, which goes back to the time of Chaucer), while others are comparative babies (for example, *go commando*) that have rapidly gained a wide currency with the help of modern technology such as television and the Internet. The stories behind the phrases reflect the full range of human experience, from work and play (*pie in the sky*, *turn the tables*) to war and death (*beat a hasty retreat*, *kick the bucket*). Some areas of activity (such as sport and seafaring) have been especially successful at lending their specialized expressions to general use. These and other particularly fruitful areas such as the Bible and Shakespeare's plays have been given their own special panels in this book. Each panel gathers together a selection of phrases to illustrate in more detail the significant impact their subject has had on the English language. Apart from the panels, the arrangement of the phrases is alphabetical: each phrase has its own entry listed alphabetically by the key word (this is the part of the phrase that doesn't vary, usually the first noun). Each entry contains a brief definition followed by an account of the phrase's history, its usage, and perhaps how it has changed over time. The thematic panels are to be found at (or close to) the relevant alphabetical point for the panel's title. An extensive thematic index is also included at the end of the book, grouping phrases according to common themes or subjects.

The Real McCoy could not have been produced without the help of Sara Hawker, and my grateful thanks are due to her for her invaluable advice and comments and particularly for the sourcing and selection of the bulk of the illustrative quotations featured in the text.

A1

excellent; first-class

This informal expression has an interesting origin. It was in fact first used in 1775 in the official publication of *Lloyd's Register*, a society founded to inspect and classify merchant ships in the interests of preserving life and property at sea. The organization has produced an annual classified list of sea-going merchant ships of a certain tonnage, called *Lloyd's Register of Shipping*, since 1764. In this list *A1* was used as a means of identifying a ship whose hull (indicated by 'A') and equipment—mast, rigging, anchors, and cables (indicated by '1')—were found on inspection to be in first-class condition; the classification has since been superseded by *100A1*. The name of the organization itself comes from the London coffee house of one Edward Lloyd, where underwriters and merchants congregated to transact business from the late 17th century.

aid and abet

help and encourage someone to do something wrong

The verb *abet* comes from an Old French term that meant 'encourage a hound to bite'. The English word dates back to the late 14th century and originally had the meaning of urging someone to do something, either good or bad. It is now only used disapprovingly and is found almost exclusively in the phrase *aid and abet*.

have an ace up your sleeve

have a secret resource available for use when needed

This phrase, which dates back to the early 20th century, has its origins in the world of card games. In many games the *ace* is the highest playing card in a suit, and a devious player intent on cheating could hide an ace up their sleeve ready to use it at an opportune moment. A North American expression with a very similar meaning is *have an ace in the hole*. This comes from the game of stud poker, in which certain cards, known as 'hole cards', are dealt face down and not turned up until all bets have been placed: a player who turns out to have an ace among their hole cards will obviously be in an advantageous position. 'An Ace in the Hole' is the title of a song by the American songwriter Cole Porter and of a 1951 film directed by Billy Wilder which explores the moral standards of the media.

hold all the aces
have all the advantages in a situation

Like *have an ace up your sleeve*, this expression comes from the role of the ace as the highest playing card in a suit. If a card player is in the happy situation of having all the aces of a pack in their hand, they are likely to be in a winning position.

within an ace of
very close to doing or achieving something

The use of *ace* in this phrase can be traced back to the oldest meaning of the word. When it first came into English, in the 14th century, *ace* referred to the side of a dice marked with one spot; it later also came to be used of the playing card in a suit bearing a single symbol. By the early 16th century the word had developed the extra meaning of 'a tiny portion or amount of something', which is the sense represented in this particular phrase.

the acid test
a situation which finally determines something's character or quality

This phrase was originally used to describe a method of testing for gold using nitric acid. Gold is resistant to the effects of nitric acid, but an object made of some other metal will show signs of corrosion if immersed in it. The expression had begun to mean 'any decisive test' by the early 20th century. In 1918 the US president Woodrow Wilson declared that 'the treatment accorded Russia by her sister nations in the months to come will be the acid test of their good will.'

across the board

involving everyone or everything

In the US, a horse-racing bet which is made *across the board* is one in which equal amounts of money are staked on the same horse to win, come second, or finish in the first three of a race. The board in question is a board at a racecourse on which bookmakers display the odds for all these different outcomes.

all-singing, all-dancing

having a large variety of impressive features

The description *all-singing, all-dancing* is now used especially of computer technology and other hi-tech gadgetry, but its roots are in a very different area of activity. The expression was originally applied to show-business acts, and may have first appeared in 1929 in a series of posters advertising the addition of sound to motion pictures. The first Hollywood musical, MGM's Oscar-winning *Broadway Melody*, was promoted with the slogan *All Talking All Singing All Dancing*.

get the all-clear

indicate or get a sign that a danger has passed

During wartime a distinctive signal or siren is sounded to indicate that a bombing raid is over and it is safe to emerge from bomb shelters or other places of refuge. This is the *all-clear*,

as opposed to the air-raid warning, which is sounded when danger is imminent. Signals such as a bugle call were first used in air raids during the First World War, a practice the comic novelist P. G. Wodehouse is referring to in this quotation from *The Inimitable Jeeves* (1923): 'The effect she had on me whenever she appeared was to make me want to slide into a cellar and lie low till they blew the All-Clear.'

run *amok*
behave uncontrollably and disruptively

The word *amok*, sometimes spelled *amuck*, comes from a Malay expression meaning 'engaging furiously in battle' or 'rushing in a state of frenzy'. It came into English via Portuguese in the mid 17th century following the growth of trading links with the East Indies, and was at first used as a noun to refer to a Malay person in a murderous frenzy. This sense is still in use, as this example from a 1977 edition of the Canadian newspaper the *Globe & Mail* illustrates: 'An apparently friendly Malay woman turns out to be an amok.' The phrase *run amok* itself dates from the late 17th century.

up the *ante*
increase what is at stake, especially in a conflict

This expression has its origins in the world of card games and gambling. Originally a Latin word meaning 'before', *ante* was first used as a noun in English by American poker players in the early 19th century, to refer to a stake put up by a player to start the betting before the cards are drawn. To 'up' (or less commonly 'raise') the ante is to put up a higher stake than your opponent, so putting more pressure on them. A 1994 edition of the *Sunday Times* posed the question: 'By his decision to up the ante in the trade war with Japan, has President Bill Clinton shot himself in the foot?'

go *ape*
become violently excited or angry

This informal phrase originated in North American air force slang in the 1950s; it's also found in the longer (but ruder) form *go ape shit*. Its roots probably lie in the 1933 film *King Kong*, which features a giant ape-like monster rampaging through New York causing widespread death and destruction. *Go ape* follows the pattern of several other expressions meaning 'become angry', such as *go ballistic* and *go bananas*.

A recent addition to their number is *go postal*, an American term which originated in various incidents involving employees of the US postal service who, apparently suffering from extreme stress, flew into a murderous rage and shot their colleagues.

the apple of your eye
someone of whom you are extremely fond or proud

When it was first used in Old English, this was a literal term for the pupil of the eye. In those pre-scientific times, the pupil was believed to be a round, solid object whose shape was similar to that of an apple. The pupil and the faculty of sight it provides are of course extremely precious, and the term was soon also applied to a person who was greatly treasured or valued. By the mid 19th century the original sense had died out, leaving only the 'cherished person' sense in use. In 2004 the phrase featured in the headlines of show-business and celebrity magazines, such as the following example from *Hello*, following the birth of the actress Gwyneth Paltrow's daughter, Apple: 'Gwyneth takes the Apple of her eye for a stroll.'

an arm and a leg
a lot of money

This expression usually occurs in one of two versions: *cost an arm and a leg* or *charge an arm and a leg*. Both are relatively modern uses, with the earliest examples dating from the 1950s, but

continues on page 10

ANIMALS

Animals have always formed a part of people's daily lives, whether as a source of food, labour, or companionship, and their prominent role is reflected in the many phrases in which they feature.

Man's best friend?

Dogs are probably the star turn in terms of the sheer number of different phrases. They have been used as working animals over the centuries and the consequences of their labours are a common theme in many expressions. **Dog tired**, *meaning 'utterly exhausted', conjures up the image of a dog worn out after a long day's hunting or rounding up sheep. The harsh treatment meted out to dogs is behind the phrase* **a dog's life**, *used to describe a miserable existence full of problems and hardship.* **A dog's dinner** *or* **breakfast**, *meaning 'a poor or messy piece of work', comes from the image of a dish of jumbled-up scraps of food given to a dog. The supposed fierce or aggressive character typical of a dog also crops up in several expressions, notably in* **dog eat dog**, *which refers to an intensely competitive situation in which both sides are willing to stoop to anything in order to succeed.* **A dog in the manger** *is a someone who stops others from having something they don't need themselves: the phrase comes from a fable telling the story of a dog that lay in a feeding trough to stop an ox and a horse from eating the hay it contained.*

Feline friends

Dogs aren't the only animals to behave aggressively. The traditional animosity between dogs and cats is behind the phrase

fight like cat and dog, which is used of two people who are continually arguing with each other. Cats are also noted for their hunting prowess and were often kept in households for the specific purpose of keeping down the mouse population. This role is reflected in the saying **while the cat's away, the mice will play**, which observes that people will naturally take advantage of the absence of someone in authority to do as they like. The relationship between cats and mice also features in another expression. If you **play cat and mouse with someone** you are using a series of cunning ploys designed alternately to encourage and thwart them, in the way that a cat toys with a mouse, pretending to release it and then pouncing on it again.

The flea's eyebrows?

The physical features of animals have also prompted a number of expressions. **The cat's whiskers** is the only survivor of a group of American slang terms for an outstanding person or thing coined back in the 1920s: others included **the flea's eyebrows** and **the canary's tusks**! Similar phrases with the same meaning in use today are **the bee's knees** and **the dog's bollocks**. **The bee's knees** was first recorded in the late 18th century and used to mean 'something very small and insignificant'. Its current sense emerged in the 1920s, probably simply following the pattern of **the cat's whiskers**. **The dog's bollocks** is a much later British invention from the 1980s, jokingly based on the same pattern. **A pig's ear**, however, has completely the opposite meaning: if you **make a pig's ear of something**, you bungle or make a mess of it. This phrase comes from the old saying 'you can't make a silk purse out of a sow's ear', meaning that you can't turn something inferior into something of top quality. The expression **for donkey's years** belongs in the category of animals' body parts too, though you might not think so at first glance. In fact it conceals a pun referring to the length of a donkey's ears and playing on an old way of pronouncing 'years' as 'ears'.

there are no definite clues as to their origin. One suggestion is that the phrase has an artistic background. In the days before photography, the only way that people could have their likeness captured would have been in a portrait by a professional painter. The pose adopted by the sitter might well affect the complexity (and therefore cost) of the painting: if both arms and legs were visible, this would cost more than if the subject was, for example, sitting at a desk with their legs hidden. The problem with this account is the discrepancy between the dates of the first recorded examples and the time when portrait painting was at its height. A more prosaic (but more plausible) explanation is simply the idea that arms and legs are very precious to an individual.

turn to ashes in your mouth

become bitterly disappointing

The origins of this phrase can be traced back to medieval times. A 14th-century work claiming to be an account of the author's travels in the East describes a legendary fruit known as the Dead Sea fruit, sometimes also referred to as the apple of Sodom. Although it apparently had a very attractive and appetizing appearance, it was said to turn to smoke and ashes if anyone tried to eat it. The expression is often found simply as *turn to ashes*, as in this account of a 1999 football match between Manchester United and the Italian side Juventus: 'The Old Trafford manager's dreams of continental domination appeared to have turned to ashes after Filippo Inzaghi's devastating double salvo.'

under the auspices of

with the help, support, or protection of

The word *auspice* originally referred to an ancient Roman way of foretelling the future: in Latin *auspicium* meant the practice of observing the flight patterns of birds in order to predict future events, a practice undertaken by a person known as an *auspex*. A decision or undertaking might be postponed if the auspex found that the omens were not favourable or 'auspicious'. This association with a favourable or successful outcome led to the word gaining the meaning 'favourable influence and patronage', and so the phrase *under the auspices of* developed. The plural *auspices* has been the usual form since the late 18th century.

back to square one

back to the starting point, with no progress made

This expression is recorded from the 1960s and, although its exact origins are uncertain, it is most likely that it comes from the world of games and sports. One suggested source is a reference to the way early radio sports commentators divided a football pitch into eight numbered sections to help the listener picture where the action was taking place. Another possibility is that it refers to a board game such as Snakes and Ladders in which the board has directions or markings indicating that a player must move forwards or backwards to a particular square. If you land on some of these squares you have to go back to the beginning or to an earlier position and start your progress all over again.

get someone's back up

make someone annoyed or angry

The image behind this expression is that of a cat arching its back when angry or threatened. The idea is recorded as early as 1728: a character in *The Provok'd Wife*, a comic play of that year by John Vanbrugh, remarks, 'How her back will be up then, when she meets me!'

a baker's dozen

thirteen

This expression, dating back to the late 16th century, arose from a practice common among bakers in former times. When selling loaves to a shopkeeper, a baker would traditionally add an extra loaf for each dozen ordered. The extra loaf represented the profit made by the shopkeeper when selling the loaves on to his customers.

*as **bald** as a coot*

completely bald

Descriptions of people as being *as bald as a coot* are recorded as far back as the 15th century. Few types of bird genuinely have no feathers on their heads, not even the bald eagle, and the coot is not one of them. Instead it has a broad white area on its forehead extending up from the base of its bill. It is possible that this may have brought to mind a bald patch at the front of a man's head, but its position on the bird's head makes this a little unlikely. A more plausible explanation lies in the history of the word *bald* itself. Words related to *bald* in other northern European languages suggest that its meaning in a prehistoric parent language was 'having a white patch or streak'. References to a *bald coot* may in fact contain evidence of this very ancient meaning, which is also represented in the English word 'piebald', used to describe a horse with a black and white coat.

jump on the **bandwagon**

join others in doing something that is suddenly popular

In American English, a *bandwagon* is a decorated wagon used to carry the band playing for a parade or procession: the term is first recorded in the mid 19th century. People very soon began to widen the scope of the word, at first especially to the world of politics. In 1899 the US statesman and later president Theodore Roosevelt wrote in a letter, 'When I once became sure of one majority they tumbled over each other to get aboard the band wagon.' Nowadays the expression is found to be appropriate to many areas of life, from computer technology to environmentalism, as the following example shows: 'When designing the elite S-class, Mercedes jumped on the green bandwagon.'

*have someone over a **barrel***

have someone at your mercy

The image conjured up by this phrase is of a powerful person subjecting a weaker one to unfair pressure. In fact, its origins lie in a situation in which someone who found themselves literally 'over a barrel' had cause to be very grateful to the other person. In the past, a person rescued from drowning would be laid face down over a barrel to help the water drain out of their lungs. It seems likely that the idea of helplessness developed into the more sinister one of coercion.

with **bated** breath

in great suspense

Bated is sometimes spelled *baited* in this phrase, but this is because of a mistaken association with the verb *bait* meaning 'put food on a hook or in a trap'. In fact *bated* here is a shortened form of the word *abated*, which means 'reduced or lessened'. The idea behind the phrase is that the anxiety or excitement you experience while waiting for something to happen is so great that you almost stop breathing.

full of **beans**

lively; in high spirits

This expression dates back to the 19th century and originally described a horse in very good condition. In the past, beans were a staple food for horses: a particular variety of bean was grown especially as fodder for horses and cattle. Beans are high in carbohydrates and a good source of protein, so a horse that was literally 'full of beans' would be full of energy and vitality.

beat a hasty retreat

withdraw quickly to avoid something unpleasant

The original context of *beating a retreat* was the battlefield. A drummer used to beat time to keep soldiers in step when marching: during a retreat his role was especially important in keeping order in the ranks and so preventing soldiers being trampled in a mass panic.

beat about the bush

discuss a matter without coming to the point

The source of this expression is the activity of shooting or netting animals for sport or food. A hunter may engage 'beaters' to walk through the ground cover or undergrowth and strike at the bushes with long sticks to flush out birds or other animals. The main action—killing or capturing the quarry—would follow this preliminary task. Furthermore, there might not actually be any game hiding there, so a great deal of time could be spent beating at bushes with no result. The idea of the preparatory or potentially unproductive activity became extended to refer to digression or time-wasting in general.

at someone's beck and call
always having to be ready to obey someone's orders

In this phrase, a *beck* is literally 'a gesture demanding attention, such as a nod or a raising of the hand'. (The word is related to 'beckon'.) Nowadays it is rarely found outside the expression *at someone's beck and call*. The idea is that of a master or mistress gesturing to or shouting for their servant to come and attend to them at once.

bells and whistles
attractive additional features

This expression originally referred to the bells and whistles on old fairground organs. It's now mainly used in the field of computing and communications, often with rather disparaging overtones suggesting that the features or options may be attractive but have little real usefulness. The following example from *.net* magazine gives a good illustration of this: 'There's no point getting a bells-and-whistles Internet connection if all you really want to do is send the odd e-mail and read the antics going down in alt.devilbunnies Usenet newsgroup.'

below the belt
unfair or unfairly

The source of this phrase is the sport of boxing. According to the rules and regulations of boxing, originally formulated under the supervision of the ninth Marquess of Queensberry in 1867, it is unlawful for a boxer to land a punch on any part of their opponent's body below the belt. In general use, the expression is often used in response to a critical or unkind remark. Margot Asquith, political hostess and wife of the Liberal prime minister Harold Asquith, once remarked of another Liberal prime minister, Lloyd George, 'He can't see a belt without hitting below it.'

*a **big** cheese*
an important and influential person

This phrase first came into use in American slang in the 1920s. Its exact origins are not certain, but it almost certainly has no connection with food. The word *cheese* probably comes from the Urdu and Persian word *čīz*, which just means 'thing'. This is suggested by the early 19th-century British English slang expression *the cheese*, which described something considered to be first-class or extremely good. It corresponds in form to the pattern of *the thing* (as in 'It's just the thing!'), and may have been introduced into English by Ango-Indians fluent in English and Urdu. There are a number of other expressions like *big cheese*, for example *big fish*, *big gun*, *big noise*, and *big shot*. They are mainly self-explanatory, although it is not clear whether a *big fish* is something desirable to catch or a shortened form of the saying *a big fish in a small pond*.

*a clean **bill** of health*
a confirmation that someone is in good health or something is in good condition

The first uses of this expression are from the mid 17th century and refer to the conditions on board a ship. The master of a ship about to sail from a port where various infectious diseases were known to be common would be given an official certificate or *bill of health* before leaving. If he was given a *clean bill of health* it confirmed that there was no infection either on board the ship or in the port. Without such a certificate the ship was unlikely to be allowed to dock at the next port on the voyage.

***birds** of a feather*
people with similar tastes and interests

The source of this phrase is the proverb *birds of a feather flock together*: the word 'a' here means 'one' or 'the same'. The idea of birds of the same species congregating or living together as a group developed into the observation that people with similar tastes and interests tend to seek each other out. It's likely that the ultimate origins of the proverb are to be found in the Bible: the Apocrypha (Ecclesiasticus 27:9) contains the line 'the birds will resort unto their like'. The phrase was used as the title of a popular BBC TV comedy series, originally broadcast between 1989 and 1998, featuring sisters whose husbands were both in prison.

give someone the bird
boo or jeer at someone

The earliest version of this expression is *the big bird*, used by people working in the theatre in the early 1800s. *The big bird* referred to was a goose, a bird well known for its aggressive hissing when threatened or annoyed. The booing and hissing of the audience at an actor's perceived poor performance might well have suggested a flock of angry geese. The idea of *giving someone the big bird* then developed, after which the phrase soon lost the word *big* and so any clue to the identity of the bird in question. The verb 'to goose' has also been recorded in the same sense, giving an even clearer link to the image behind the idioms.

strictly for the birds
not worth considering; unimportant

This phrase dates back to the 1950s and was first used as a slang term by American soldiers. It is likely that it referred to the way in which some birds peck at the droppings of horses and cattle: using the expression of something regarded as unworthy of consideration would be a euphemistic way of avoiding other ruder and less acceptable references to excrement!

bite the bullet
face up to doing something difficult or unpleasant

Before the development of anaesthetics wounded soldiers undergoing surgery on the battlefield would be given a bullet or some other hard object to bite on to prevent them from crying out or harming themselves when the pain became unbearable. This practice gave rise to the sense of stoically avoiding showing fear or distress, and from this came the current meaning of facing up to something unpleasant, as in this example from *The Sun*: 'So bite the bullet. Tell your fiancée you're sorry to hurt her but that you've realized it would be a mistake to marry.'

be in someone's black books

be out of favour with someone

Black book has been used since the 15th century to refer to various types of official book bound in black cloth or leather, especially those used to note down misdemeanours and the punishments meted out to their perpetrators. The relevant books here are probably the black-bound books in which Henry VIII's commissioners officially recorded accounts of scandals and corruption within the English monasteries in the 1530s. The monasteries and specifically the Church of Rome were very much out of favour with Henry because of the Pope's refusal to annul Henry's marriage to his first wife, Catherine of Aragon. These books provided the evidence to support Henry's plan of breaking with the Pope and the Church of Rome, allowing him to dissolve the monasteries (and benefit from their wealth) and marry Anne Boleyn.

black box

a flight recorder in an aircraft

The first use of *black box* is as RAF slang for a navigational instrument in an aircraft which allowed the pilot and crew to locate bombing targets in poor visibility. The phrase has nothing to do with the colour of the device, and in fact alludes to its mystifying nature. The notion behind it was that only experts in the field of aviation would understand how the equipment worked. To a non-expert it would have seemed very mysterious and almost magical—or 'black magical'! The current meaning of 'an aircraft's flight recorder' also encompasses the idea of magical power. The flight recorder contains all the information from the aeroplane's instruments and so in the event of a crash can reveal vital clues as to its cause. The phrase has also been extended to any piece of equipment whose workings are a mystery to most users.

blaze a trail

be the first to do something; be a pioneer

The actual origins of this phrase are quite different to the image first conjured up. Initially you might think that it comes from the activity of clearing a way through scrubland by setting fire to it, but this is not the case. The expression in fact comes from another meaning of the word *blaze*, namely 'a white spot or mark on an animal's face'. *Blazing a trail* literally involves chipping off bits of bark from trees to expose a pale area (or 'blaze') of wood beneath, thereby showing the route you have taken to those following behind. Incidentally, *blaze* meaning 'white mark' and *blaze* meaning 'a fiercely burning fire' may in fact be related to each other, as both incorporate an idea of brightness or whiteness.

turn a **blind** eye
pretend not to notice something

A clue to the origins of this phrase lies in the less common alternative *turn a Nelson eye*. The British admiral and naval hero Horatio Nelson had lost the sight in his right eye during the siege of Calvi in 1794 but it was in allusion to reports of his actions at the Battle of Copenhagen in 1801 that the phrase first came into use. During the attack on the Danes, Nelson's superior, Sir Hyde Parker, feared that his men would suffer very heavy losses and so hoisted the signal for Nelson to halt his attack and withdraw. However, Nelson avoided seeing the signal by putting a telescope to his blind eye and continued the battle. An hour later he was victorious, with British casualties around six times fewer than those on the Danish side.

make your **blood** run cold OR curdle
terrify you

These two phrases have their origins in medieval theories of physiology and medicine. At that time the human body was thought to be made up of four main fluids or 'humours': blood, phlegm, choler (or 'yellow bile'), and melancholy (or 'black bile'). These fluids were believed to determine someone's appearance and temperament according to the relative proportions in which they were present in the body. According to this system, blood was the hot, moist element. Extreme fear or horror would cause it to become cold or even to curdle (or solidify), so stopping it from doing its job of supplying the body with vital heat and energy. The theory is also reflected in the phrase *in cold blood* meaning 'without feeling or mercy'. Here, the idea is that the blood was in an unnaturally cold state compared with the normal hot-blooded state characteristic of an act of passion or violence. The opposite situation is represented in the phrase *make your blood boil*, meaning 'infuriate or anger you greatly'. The image behind this was that of the blood becoming too hot as a result of a dangerous overreaction to some strong emotion.

blow *hot and cold*
keep changing your mind

The source of this phrase is the tale of the man and the satyr, one of the famous fables of Aesop, a Greek storyteller of the 6th century BC. In the story, a traveller lost in a forest encounters a satyr (a type of woodland god). The satyr offers him lodging for the night, promising to lead him safely out of the woods in the morning. On the way to the satyr's home the man blows on his hands. The satyr asks him why he does this, to which he replies, 'My breath warms my cold hands.' At the satyr's home they sit down to eat some steaming hot porridge. The man blows on his first spoonful and again the satyr asks him why. 'The porridge is too hot to eat and my breath will cool it,' he answers. At this the satyr orders him to leave, saying 'I can have nothing to do with a man who can blow hot and cold with the same breath.' Although the tale itself is centuries old, the English expression dates back only as far as the late 16th century.

out of the **blue**
without warning; very
unexpectedly

The related expression *a bolt from the blue*, meaning 'a sudden unexpected event or piece of news',

gives a clearer hint as to the image behind both these phrases. The *bolt* referred to is a bolt of lightning and the *blue* is a clear blue sky. The idea encapsulated in the phrases is that you would expect to have warning of an imminent thunderstorm by dark storm clouds massing above: thunder and lightning from a blue sky would be completely unexpected.

call someone's bluff

challenge someone to carry out a stated intention

In the 19th century the card game poker was called *bluff*, probably from the way a player had to *bluff*, or try to deceive, the others as to how good their hand of cards really was. *Calling someone's bluff* meant making another player show their hand in order to reveal that its value was weaker than their heavy betting had suggested. From this developed the sense of challenging anything you suspect to be false or mere bravado.

Bob's your uncle

everything is fine; problem solved

The exact origins of this phrase are uncertain, although it is often said to have been coined following a controversial government appointment in 1887. Arthur Balfour, who was only 39 at the time, was given the important post of Chief Secretary for Ireland by his uncle Lord Salisbury, the then prime minister. Lord Salisbury's first name was Robert, which is of course the full form of the name *Bob*. The problem with this suggestion is that the earliest recorded examples do not appear until the 1930s, around fifty years after the incident in question. This may reflect the limitations of the evidence, however: the phrase is often said while performing a task, describing how easy it is to do, and so may have been largely restricted to speech.

make no bones about something

have no hesitation in saying or doing something

Dating back to the 16th century, this expression has a gastronomic source. The image behind it is of someone eating a bowl of soup with no bones in it: not having to pick out bones or worry about swallowing any would make the soup much easier to eat. This quickly led to the idea of doing or saying something readily and without restraint. An erstwhile television presenter, interviewed in *The Independent* in 2001, remarked: 'I make no bones about it. I'm not at all politically correct.'

to boot

as well; in addition

The *boot* in this expression is not the sort you wear on your feet. In fact, it is an old word meaning 'good, advantage, or profit' which dates back to the 10th century. It had died out in these senses by the 19th

century and only survives in this phrase and in the related adjective
bootless (rarely used today) meaning 'ineffectual or useless'.

pull yourself up by your (own) bootstraps

improve your position or status by your own efforts

A *bootstrap* is a short strip of folded leather sewn into the back of a boot to help you pull it on more easily. The idea of bootstraps as symbolizing a person's own efforts may have come from the fact that, while wealthy people had servants at their disposal to help them dress, a person with a lower social status would have to do everything themselves, including pulling on their own boots. In the 1950s the phrase found its way into the world of computing, in the term *bootstrapping*, now shortened to the more familiar *booting* or *booting up*. This refers to the process of loading a program into a computer that will then trigger the start-up program.

borrowed plumes

a pretentious display that doesn't belong to you

The source of this expression is the fable of the jay and the peacock by Aesop, a Greek storyteller of the 6th century BC. In this tale a jay finds a number of peacock feathers lying on the ground. He ties them to his own tail and struts about proudly, pretending to be a peacock. However, when the other peacocks realize his trick they peck and pull at the offending feathers, and the jay departs hastily in shame. When he returns to the other jays, who have been watching the whole business, they observe angrily that 'it is not only fine feathers that make fine birds'. This fable also gave rise to the proverb *fine feathers make fine birds*, meaning 'an eye-catching appearance makes someone seem impressive'.

have a lot of bottle

be bold or show initiative

This and the related phrases *lose your bottle* and *bottle out*, meaning 'lose your nerve', date back to the 1950s. This use of *bottle* probably comes from a mid 19th-century slang expression *no bottle*, meaning 'no good, useless' (the reason for this is not clear). Another suggested source is the rhyming slang phrase *bottle and glass*, meaning 'arse'. 'Arse' is of course an informal term for someone's buttocks or bottom, and an old meaning of the word *bottom* was 'courage or strength of character'.

BIBLICAL EXPRESSIONS

The Christian Church has had a very influential role in people's lives over the centuries, and it is not surprising that biblical references are a significant feature in English phrases, even if nowadays many people are unaware of their origins.

Setting a bad example

Biblical characters are represented in several expressions. From the Old Testament we have **a Job's comforter**, meaning 'a person who makes someone more distressed while seeming to comfort them'. Job was a wealthy man whose patience and piety were tested by a series of undeserved misfortunes, and whose friends' attempts to comfort him only added to his sense of despair. Jesus's disciples also feature in a number of expressions. **A Judas kiss** is an act of betrayal, especially when it is disguised as an act of friendship. It comes from the account of Judas Iscariot's betrayal of Jesus to the authorities, in which he identified Jesus to the soldiers coming to arrest him by greeting him with a kiss. Someone who refuses to believe something without having absolute proof may be called **a doubting Thomas**. This refers to the story of the Apostle Thomas, who declared that he would not believe that Christ had risen from the dead until he had seen and touched his wounds.

The right course

Many of the parables and teachings in the Bible have given rise to familiar phrases. We use the expression **a good Samaritan** to refer to a charitable or helpful person, after the man from Samaria who stopped to help a traveller who had been beaten and robbed. The phrase **a prodigal son** is used to describe someone who leaves home to lead an extravagant lifestyle but later returns full of repentance. The same story gave rise to the phrase **killing the fatted calf**, meaning 'produce a lavish celebratory feast', in reference to the forgiving response of the father on the return of his wayward son. Punishment and forgiveness are themes that crop up in other phrases too. If you **rule someone with a rod of iron** you keep very strict or harsh control over them. This expression comes from Psalm 2:9: 'Thou shalt break them with a rod of iron; thou shalt dash them in pieces like a potter's vessel.' **Turn the other cheek**, on the other hand, means 'refrain from retaliating when you have been attacked or insulted', after the advice given by Jesus in Matthew 5:39: 'Whosoever shall smite thee on thy right cheek, turn to him the other also.'

Everyday sayings

There are several idioms whose links with the Bible are less obvious. Nowadays we often hear the phrase **go the extra mile**, especially from politicians trying to assure us that every effort will be made in the attempt to achieve something. This can be traced back to Matthew 5:41: 'And whosoever shall compel thee to go a mile, go with him twain.' **At the eleventh hour**, meaning 'at the latest possible moment', comes from the parable of the labourers who were hired right at the end of the day to work in the vineyard. If you **wash your hands of something**, you disclaim responsibility for it: this refers to the description of Pontius Pilate washing his hands before the crowd after he was forced to condemn Jesus to death. The expression **credit where credit is due** means 'praise should be given when it is deserved, even when you are reluctant to do so'. The sentiment occurred earlier in the form 'honour where honour is due', following Romans 13:7 in the 1611 King James Bible: 'Render therefore to all their dues: tribute to whom tribute is due; custom to whom custom; fear to whom fear; honour to whom honour.'

a shot across the bows
a warning statement or gesture

This phrase has its origins in the world of naval warfare. A shot fired across the bows of a ship is one which is not intended to hit it but to make it stop or alter its course. Back in 2000 the Debt Advice Bureau announced prophetically: 'The first rise in base rates since 10th February 2000 is no more than a warning shot across the bows of the British consumer. Increasing the base rate from 3.50% to 3.75% is a signal that rates can rise and will rise if need be.'

brass monkey
used to refer to extremely cold weather

Brass monkey comes from the mid 20th-century slang expression *cold enough to freeze the balls off a brass monkey*. The origins of this are not certain, but the best-known explanation traces its roots back to the days of sailing ships and cannons. In former times, warships would be equipped with cannons firing heavy iron cannonballs. Each cannon needed its own supply of cannonballs, which would be stacked next to it on special trays. The trays had indentations to stop the cannonballs from rolling around and were known as 'monkeys'. They had to be made of brass to stop the iron cannonballs from rusting on to them, but using brass created another problem in cold weather. Brass contracts much more quickly and to a greater degree than iron at low temperatures, and so in freezing conditions the indentations in the trays would be insufficient to hold the cannonballs securely and they would roll off. There are some problems with this explanation. Firstly, it would have to be extremely cold to cause sufficient contraction in the metal for this to happen. Secondly, the earliest recorded versions of the phrase (dating from the mid 19th century) feature noses and tails rather than balls, suggesting rather a reference to a brass statue of a monkey.

brave new world
a new and hopeful period resulting from major changes in society

Use of this phrase is generally coloured by the fact that Aldous Huxley chose it as the ironic title of his 1932 novel about a futuristic utopia or ideal world. The setting of the novel is the distant future, in which the World Controllers have created a 'perfect' society using genetic engineering, brainwashing, and other ploys to manipulate the masses. Regarded as one of the most important novels of the 20th century, the story focuses on the dissatisfaction of one person, Bernard Marx, with the claustrophobic restrictions and demands and on his wish to break free. Huxley borrowed the phrase from Shakespeare's *The Tempest*. On first encountering other human beings, Miranda (brought up in isolation on an island) exclaims: 'How many goodly creatures are there here! How beauteous mankind is! O brave new world, That has such people in't.'

step into the breach

take the place of someone who is suddenly unable to do a job

The origins of this expression lie in battles and sieges. In military terms, a *breach* is a gap in fortifications made by enemy guns or explosives. Defending soldiers would have to rush to position themselves in the breach and attempt to prevent the stronghold from being overrun by the enemy's attacking forces. From this the idea developed of a person in any sort of job suddenly having to take over from another in an emergency.

bread and circuses

a diet of entertainment or policies provided to keep the masses happy and docile

Bread and circuses is a translation of Latin *panem et circenses*, which appeared in the work of the Roman satirist Juvenal, (1st century AD). He was referring to the way in which Roman emperors would organize gladiatorial games and handouts of grain to the people in order to deflect their attention from the conditions of poverty and hardship they endured. The English phrase is recorded from the early 20th century, but the Latin version was used in English contexts as far back as the 18th century.

in a brown study

absorbed in your thoughts

The 'study' in question here is not a room for reading or working in, but a state of daydreaming or meditation, a meaning that has long been out of use in English. But why 'brown'? In Anglo-Saxon times, the word simply meant 'dark'; limitation to the distinct colour we are now familiar with did not occur until the medieval period. The idea of darkness developed into a further sense of 'gloomy or serious', and this is the sense that occurs in *a brown study*.

DANVILLE PUBLIC LIBRARY
DANVILLE, INDIANA

pass the buck

shift the responsibility to someone else

In the card game poker a *buck* is an object placed as a reminder in front of a player whose turn it is deal. If you *pass the buck* you hand over the job of dealing to the next player. A related expression is *the buck stops here*, meaning that the responsibility or blame for something cannot or should not be passed to someone else. The US president Harry S. Truman famously had this as the wording of a sign on his desk, indicating that the ultimate responsibility for running the country lay with him.

in the buff

naked

The word *buff* originally meant 'a buffalo or other type of wild ox', and buff leather, often shortened to simply *buff*, was leather made from the hide of such an animal (usually an ox). This leather was very strong, with a fuzzy surface and a pale yellowish-beige colour. It was used to make military uniforms and so soldiers would be described as 'wearing buff' or 'in buff'. The combination of these descriptions and the similarity of the leather's colour to that of human skin led to its use as a term for 'the bare skin' in the mid 17th century. A related expression is *strip to the buff*.

bully for you!

well done! good for you!

This phrase, which is generally used ironically, is not directly connected to the familiar sense of *bully*, i.e. 'an aggressive person who intimidates weaker people'. Instead, it employs an informal American use of the word to mean 'excellent or first-rate'. When it came into the English language in the 16th century, *bully* was a term of endearment, much like 'sweetheart' or 'darling', and it then became an informal way of addressing a male friend. By the end of the 17th century it was being used as an adjective to mean 'admirable or jolly', and finally the more general sense of 'first-rate' developed, a sense which today survives only in the expression *bully for you*.

go a bundle on
be very keen or fond of

The origins of this expression lie in the world of betting and horse racing. *Bundle* is a slang term first used in the US in the early 20th century for 'a large sum of money'. If you *go a bundle on a horse* you bet a lot of money on it because you fancy it very strongly to win. The idea of 'fancying' something soon became extended from horse racing to more general contexts. The phrase is usually found in the negative, to refer to something you are not very keen on, as in 'He never drank and certainly didn't go a bundle on gambling.'

burn your boats OR bridges
commit yourself irrevocably to a course of action

In a military campaign, burning the boats or bridges used to reach a particular position would mean that you had destroyed any means of escape or retreat: you had no choice but to fight on.

go for a Burton
meet with disaster; be ruined, destroyed, or killed

This phrase first appears in RAF slang in the 1940s, when it was used to mean 'be killed in a crash'. Its exact origins remain rather mysterious. One suggestion is that *Burton* referred to a British men's clothing firm of that name, with a *Burton* being a Burton's suit. Another proposal is that *going for a Burton* meant going for a pint of Burton's beer. The second theory seems the more plausible as there is no independent evidence of *Burton* alone meaning 'a suit', and no known record of *go for a Burton's suit*, as you might expect if this were the origin of the phrase. On the other hand, *Burton* is recorded from the mid 19th century as a term for a type of beer made in Burton upon Trent, in Staffordshire (the town is still famous for its brewing industry), while 'going for a beer' is possibly more believable as a gentle euphemism for dying than 'going for a suit'.

bury the hatchet
end a quarrel or conflict

The source of this expression is a Native American custom which involved burying a hatchet or tomahawk to mark the conclusion of a peace treaty between warring groups. The tomahawk, as the warriors' main weapon, symbolized war, and so burying it indicated that a conflict was truly over. The custom is described as early as 1680; the current sense of the phrase emerged around seventy years later. In 1974 the then prime minister Harold Wilson observed wryly of his Cabinet: 'I've buried all the hatchets. But I know where I've buried them and I can dig them up if necessary.'

by and large
on the whole; with everything considered

This phrase was originally nautical, and described the handling of a ship in different wind conditions. If a ship was *by the wind* it meant that it was sailing as close to the direction of the wind as possible. If the ship *had the wind large* it meant that the wind was crossing the direction of the ship's course in a favourable direction. The expression moved into general use in the early 18th century, but an awareness of the original context remained for some time. In *The Innocents Abroad* (1869) the American humorist Mark Twain wrote: 'Taking it "by and large", as the sailors say, we had a pleasant . . . run.'

C

the whole (kit and) caboodle
the whole lot; everything or everyone

This informal expression was first recorded in the US in the mid 19th century, and soon spread to British English. It combines and extends several phrases with much the same meaning. *The whole kit*, meaning 'the whole lot', is recorded from the late 18th century and was expanded to *the whole kit and boodle*, 'boodle' being another word meaning 'a lot' or 'a crowd'. 'Caboodle' is either a shortened version of 'kit and boodle' or an alteration of 'boodle' to make a catchy phrase together with 'kit'. Similar expressions in existence in the 19th century included *the whole kit and boiling* and *the whole kit and cargo*, but these seem to have completely passed out of use.

Caesar's wife
a person who should be above suspicion

This phrase has its origins in Julius Caesar's decision to divorce his wife Pompeia, as recounted by the Greek biographer Plutarch. Publius Clodius, a well-known womanizer, smuggled himself into the house where the women of Caesar's household were celebrating a festival. This caused a great scandal, but Caesar refused to bring any charges against Clodius, instead deciding to divorce Pompeia. When questioned about his decision he replied, 'I thought my wife ought not even to be under suspicion.'

in cahoots
working or conspiring together dishonestly

The earliest examples of this phrase are found from the early 19th century in the south and west of the US. Originally the sense was neutral, meaning 'in partnership', as in 'he wished me to go in cahoots in a store'. Nowadays, however, the word is almost always used with connotations of dishonesty and conspiracy, as in this example from the *Chicago Times*: 'The area is dominated by Shining Path guerrillas in cahoots with drug traffickers.' The source of *cahoot* is by no means certain. Some have suggested that it comes from French *cahute*, meaning 'a cabin': like the English word *cabin* itself, this once had the meaning of a political cabinet, a group of senior ministers who control government policy. Another suggestion is that it is an alteration of *cohort*, with the idea of a group of people working closely together on the same enterprise.

cannot hold a candle to

is nowhere near as good as

Before the invention of gas or electric lighting, an assistant or apprentice would stand next to their master or mistress literally holding a candle to provide enough light for them to work by. *Holding a candle to someone* consequently came to mean 'help someone as a subordinate or in a menial way'. This in turn led to the development of the modern meaning which suggests that one person is so inferior to another that they are not even capable of doing this simple task.

not worth the candle

not justifiable because of the trouble or cost involved

The earliest examples of this expression, recorded from the late 17th century, show that it originated as a translation of the French phrase *le jeu ne vaut pas la chandelle*, meaning 'the game is not worth the candle'. The 'game' in question was a game of cards involving betting, which wouldn't be worth playing if the costs involved in providing the light for it (in the form of candles) would outweigh any likely winnings. The comment is now applied to any risky or uncertain enterprise seen as unlikely to bring sufficient profits or benefits.

hold all the cards

be in the strongest or most advantageous position

This is just one of many phrases in which a game of cards stands for any enterprise. The player who *holds all the cards* is guaranteed to win the game. If you *play your cards right* you might do the same, or get what you want. If you *keep your cards close to your chest* you are secretive about your plans or activities, like a card player trying to prevent others from seeing their hand. If you *show your cards* or *put your cards on the table* you are completely open about your thoughts or intentions.

on the cards
possible or likely

The *cards* referred to here may be either ordinary playing cards or tarot cards, with a North American version, *in the cards*, suggesting more clearly the particular context: namely, fortune telling. In the past both types of cards were used to tell the future, but nowadays tarot cards are the ones we usually associate with this practice. Tarot cards did in fact originate as simply another type of playing card, traditionally having seventy-eight cards with five suits in a pack, and they are still used for playing games, especially in continental Europe.

on the carpet
being severely reprimanded by someone in authority

It's a common misconception that the *carpet* in this expression refers to the familiar floor covering in, for example, a head teacher's office. But *carpet* in fact originally meant 'a table covering', and in this phrase alludes specifically to the 'carpet' of a council table. It was first used to describe a matter up for discussion at a meeting (as in the similar expression *on the table*). It was then extended to refer to the treatment of a person who had committed an offence. Historically, such a person would be summoned before the members of a council seated at their table and would there receive their official reprimand. The phrase has also given rise to the verb *to carpet someone* meaning 'reprimand someone severely'.

build **castles** in the air
daydream about unattainable schemes

The idea behind this phrase goes back many centuries to the time of St Augustine (354–430), whose writings contain the expression *subtracto fundamento in aere aedificare*, meaning 'build on air without foundation'. The earliest (and now less common) expression of this type in English was in fact *build castles in Spain*, recorded from the beginning of the 15th century. This form probably comes from the Old French phrase *châteaux en Espagne*, which dates back to the 13th century. It may have arisen because much of Spain was under Moorish control in the Middle Ages: any plan to build castles there would have had very little chance of success.

by a long **chalk**
by far

The *chalk* in this phrase and in its opposite, *not by a long chalk* meaning 'by no means, not at all', is a piece of chalk used for writing. Two possibilities have been suggested as the precise source, either the pub or the classroom. In the case of the pub, the phrase would refer to the practice of marking up points scored in a game on a blackboard. In the classroom, teachers used to award marks for merit and chalk these up on a blackboard. In either case, a long line of chalk marks against your name would mean you were way ahead of the others. This image of succeeding or doing better than other people can also be seen in the use of *chalk something up* to mean 'achieve something noteworthy, as in 'Roberts chalked up his hundredth Test wicket in the record time of two years and 144 days.'

chance your arm
boldly undertake something risky or difficult

A number of suggestions have been made regarding the precise origins of this phrase, which is recorded from the 1880s. The earliest use indicates that it was a slang term used among tailors, perhaps with the idea of rushing the job of sewing in a sleeve and so risking the stitches coming loose. Another theory suggests it is a military expression referring to the stripes on the sleeve of a uniform that indicate a soldier's rank. If a soldier undertook some illicit enterprise he might end up being demoted and so lose one of his stripes. Both these explanations have the *arm* representing a sleeve, but another proposal puts the person's actual arm at risk. This suggestion links the phrase with a famous event in Irish history. In 1492 the Ormond and Kildare families were engaged in a bitter feud. After one battle the Earl of Ormond and his men fled to St Patrick's cathedral in Dublin. His opponent, the Earl of Kildare, decided that the time had come to end the fighting and make peace. Wishing to show his sincerity, he bravely cut a hole in the cathedral's door and put his arm through. Fortunately, the Earl of Ormond accepted his offer of reconciliation and shook his hand rather than cutting it off! Although this last explanation is the most colourful, the fact that the events described happened so long before any record of the phrase makes it rather unlikely to be true.

chase the dragon

take heroin by heating it and inhaling the fumes through a tube of paper

This expression is believed to have originated as a translation of a Chinese phrase. Dragons often feature in Chinese mythology, and the idea behind the phrase is that the undulating movements of fumes rising from the tinfoil in which the drug is heated resemble those of the tail of a dragon. By constantly moving the tube of paper over the tinfoil to follow the fumes, the user manages to inhale as much of the drug as possible.

an old *chestnut*

a frequently retold joke or story

The source of this phrase, which is first recorded in the 1880s, is probably a play called *The Broken Sword*, written by William Dimond in 1816. In one scene there is an exchange between two of the characters, Zavior and Pablo. Zavior is in the middle of telling a story, saying: 'When suddenly from the thick boughs of a cork tree—'. At this point Pablo jumps in with: 'A chestnut, Captain, a chestnut . . . Captain, this is the twenty-seventh time I have heard you relate this story, and you invariably said, a chestnut, till now.' There are some doubts as to the truth of this explanation, but nothing more plausible has been suggested.

a *chip* off the old block

someone who resembles one of their parents in character or behaviour

The basis of this expression is the image of a small piece cut off a larger block of wood: the *chip* removed will retain the qualities of the larger block, such as hardness or fineness of grain. The phrase dates back to the early 17th century, originally in the forms *chip of the same block* and *chip of the old block*. A famous example is found in a remark made by the politician Edmund Burke in 1781. Commenting on Pitt the Younger's maiden speech in Parliament, he observed that he was 'not merely a chip of the old "block", but the old block itself'.

a *chip* on your shoulder

a deeply ingrained grievance or resentment

This phrase is first recorded in American English in the mid 19th century. An explanation of why a chip of wood should come to be on a person's shoulder featured in the *Long Island Telegraph* newspaper dated 20 May 1830. A practice prevalent among boys spoiling for a fight was described: 'When two churlish boys were *determined* to fight, a *chip* would be placed on the shoulder of one, and the other demanded to knock it off at his peril.'

Hobson's *choice*

a choice of taking what is offered or nothing

This expression dates from the mid 17th century. It comes from the name of one Thomas Hobson (1554–1631), a man who hired out horses in Cambridge. He refused to allow his customers their own choice of horse from the stables, but insisted on hiring them out in strict rotation: a customer was offered the 'choice' of the horse nearest the door or none at all. Perhaps one of the best modern examples of a case of *Hobson's choice* was Henry Ford's remark about the choice of colours available for the new Model T car: 'Any colour—so long as it's black.'

Since the mid 20th century the phrase *Hobson's choice* has gained a new meaning: it's also used as rhyming slang for 'voice'.

chop and change

change your opinions or behaviour repeatedly and abruptly

Both *chop* and *change* once had the meaning 'barter or exchange', and from the 15th century onwards they were often used together in this alliterative phrase. At first it meant 'buy and sell', but over time the perception that *chop* had any independent meaning outside the phrase became lost and 'change' came to be interpreted in its more usual sense. The modern use, with *chop* merely reinforcing the idea of abruptness, is recorded as early as the mid 16th century.

close but no cigar

almost but not quite successful

This expression, mainly used in North American English, may have originated as a comment to a losing competitor in a contest of strength. In contests such as arm-wrestling a cigar was often awarded to the winner. An opponent who had come very close to winning, having put up a good effort, might well have been consoled with this remark. The phrase has spread to British English, as shown in this example from the novel *High Fidelity* by Nick Hornby (1995): 'But, you know . . . you did not represent my last and best chance of a relationship. So, you know, nice try. Close, but no cigar.'

like the clappers

very fast or very hard

The word *clapper* can refer to a number of different objects used for striking something. The most likely candidate for this phrase is either the striking part of a bell or a device in a mill for striking or shaking the hopper to make the grain move down to the millstones. Both a set of pealing bells and a mill in full operation would have their clappers moving very fast. The expression *like the clappers* was first found in RAF slang in the 1940s, often in the extended form *like the clappers of hell*.

COLOURS

Many English expressions feature colours, which have been traditionally associated with particular emotions, qualities, and customs.

A whiter shade of pale

The colour white has long represented the qualities of purity, innocence, or virtue and this is the image behind **whiter than white** meaning 'morally beyond reproach'. **A white knight** is a company that makes a welcome bid for a company facing a hostile takeover bid. The phrase comes from the traditional character in gleaming armour found in tales of chivalry, who rides to the rescue of damsels in distress. Continuing the theme of goodies and baddies, the good characters in cowboy films traditionally wear white hats while the villains' headgear is black.

Dark deeds

Not surprisingly, as the opposite of white, black is often linked with wickedness, or at least bad behaviour! The **black sheep** of a family is someone who is regarded as a disgrace to it because of their scandalous conduct. If someone describes you as **not so black as you are painted**, it means that you're not as bad as you're said to be. It comes from the 16th-century proverb 'the devil is not as black as he is painted', which warned against basing your fears of something on exaggerated reports. Black doesn't always have bad connotations, however, as demonstrated by the phrase **in the black** meaning 'not owing any money'. Here, black simply refers to the colour of the ink used for writing the credit part of financial accounts, as contrasted with the red ink which was traditionally used for debit items and balances to ensure that they stood out on the page and received the necessary attention.

It's from this practice that we get the opposite phrase **in the red**, meaning 'in debt or overdrawn'.

A fiery temper

The colour red has long been connected with anger and violence, probably because of its association with blood. If you **see red** you suddenly become very angry; people also talk about a **red mist** in front of their eyes. Similarly, **a red rag to a bull** is something said, done, or seen which is certain to provoke or anger someone. This comes from the idea that red was traditionally supposed to provoke a bull, and of course the capes used by matadors in bullfighting are red. A more concrete link with violence can be found in expressions such as **caught red-handed**. The image here is of a murderer caught with their hands covered in the blood of their victim, but over time it's been diluted to mean simply 'discovered in or just after the act of doing something wrong'.

The blues

Blue has a mixture of associations, both bad and good. If you're **feeling blue** or **have the blues** you're unhappy or depressed. This phrase probably arose from the appearance of the skin when someone has had a shock or is very cold, both rather miserable situations. On the positive side, however, we have **true blue**, a phrase with rather complicated origins. It can mean both 'real or genuine' or 'staunchly loyal'. In the first sense, it's likely that it developed from the expression **blue blood**, which referred to someone of noble birth. This was a translation of Spanish 'sangre azul' and was used of the oldest aristocratic families of the former Spanish kingdom of Castile, who claimed to have no Moorish or other foreign ancestors. It probably arose from fact that veins are more visible in fair-skinned people than in those with darker skin. The second sense of **true blue** may have come from the idea of the unchanging blue of the sky or have referred to a particular blue dye that never lost its colour. The phrase is now especially associated with the British Conservative party, partly because blue is the party colour.

see red • black sheep • a white knight • blue blood • caught red-handed

clear the decks

prepare for something by dealing with possible obstacles to progress

The origins of this phrase lie in naval warfare. Before a battle at sea sailors were required literally to clear the ship's decks of all obstacles or unwanted items that might cause a hazard during the fighting. The phrase itself is only recorded from the 19th century, but the idea of removing obstacles that might prevent progress is found three centuries earlier in the expression *clear the coast*. This refers to fighting or driving off any enemy ships or soldiers in the vicinity of a chosen landing point. It in turn developed into *the coast is clear*, meaning 'there is no danger of being observed or caught'.

in (OR out of) the closet

hiding (or no longer hiding) something, especially homosexuality

Closet is the usual North American word for a cupboard or a wardrobe, but originally it referred to a private room. The idea of privacy easily takes on the more negative associations of secrecy, or of hiding any fact that you would rather others didn't find out about. This wider sense is also found in the adjective *closet*, meaning 'secret or covert', and in the phrase *a skeleton in the closet (or cupboard)*. In 1999 Pat Buchanan, then seeking nomination as the presidential candidate for the Reform Party, observed: 'Everyone has a skeleton in their closet. The difference between Bill Clinton and myself is that he has a walk-in closet.' The phrases *in the closet* and *out of the closet*, dating from the 1960s, now almost always refer to hiding or revealing homosexuality, and the latter has in turn has given rise to the verb *to out someone*, meaning 'reveal the homosexuality of a prominent person'.

on cloud nine

extremely happy

The source of this expression is probably the classification of clouds given in a meteorological guide published in 1896 called the *International Cloud Atlas*. According to this guide there are ten basic types of cloud, number nine being the cumulonimbus. Cumulonimbus clouds form a towering fluffy mass with a flat base and sometimes a flat top, a shape that might suggest a rather comfortable cushion for reclining on. The first examples are from the 1950s, some with the alternative, but now dated variant *on cloud seven*. This version prompts a different possible explanation, namely the phrase *in seventh heaven*, which has the same meaning but occurs more than a hundred years earlier. The *seven heavens* feature in Jewish and Muslim belief, with the highest being the abode of God and the most exalted angels.

haul someone over the coals
reprimand someone severely

The origins of this phrase lie in a form of torture that involved dragging the victim over the coals of a slow fire. The practice is first referred to in the mid 16th century, but the earliest record of the current use is in one of Horatio Nelson's dispatches in 1795. In it he remarks: 'I think the Admiral will be hauled over the coals for not letting me have ships.'

go cold turkey
abruptly and completely stop taking drugs

The side effects of the sudden withdrawal of addictive drugs include alternate bouts of shivering and sweating. Shivering is of course usually accompanied by 'goose flesh' or 'goose pimples', the bumpy condition of the skin caused by the hairs rising up. This condition is so called because it resembles the skin of a dead plucked goose—or turkey, hence the phrase *go cold turkey*.

show your true colours
reveal your real character or intentions

The distinguishing flag of a ship or regiment is known as its *colours*. A ship engaged in illegal trading or in time of war might fly a bogus flag to deceive the authorities or the enemy, and this would be known as *sailing under false colours*. If the ship *showed its true colours* it would reveal itself to be the enemy by some action such as firing its guns or fleeing. A related phrase is *nail your colours to the mast*, which means 'declare openly and firmly what you believe or support'. This comes from the idea that a ship engaged in a battle might nail its flag to the mast so that it couldn't be lowered in defeat.

go commando
wear no underpants

This expression dates back to the 1980s and early examples suggest that it originated as American college slang: its current wider use is most likely thanks to its occurrence in a 1996 episode of the popular TV sitcom *Friends*. The source of the phrase is probably the idea that the practice of not wearing underpants is common among military commandos. The custom doesn't appeal to everyone, though, as the British comedian Dave Gorman observes: 'If God had wanted men to "go commando" he wouldn't have invented polycotton with two per cent lycra! When my zip broke once I was glad to have boxers on.'

a name to conjure with
someone important in a particular field

The original sense of *conjure* was far more serious and powerful than the current meanings suggest. In the Middle Ages the word had the more sinister meaning of 'call upon a demon or spirit to appear by means of a magic ritual'. This sense is the one preserved in *a name to conjure with*, although the phrase has now lost its evil implications and merely retains the idea of power.

cook the books
alter facts or figures dishonestly or illegally

This informal expression may sound relatively modern, but in fact the word *cook* has been used to mean 'tamper with something' since the 1630s. Early examples refer to cooking 'proof' or 'accounts' (and in one notable example 'spelling'), but nowadays it is almost always 'books' that are cooked.

cook someone's goose
spoil someone's plans or cause someone's downfall

The origins of this phrase are not certain. The underlying idea may be the fact that a goose was often specially kept and fattened up to be the centrepiece of a forthcoming celebration, and of course goose is still a popular alternative to the traditional

crack 41

Christmas turkey. If someone killed and cooked the goose in advance of the special occasion it was destined for, this would spoil the plans for the meal (and might even result in severe punishment for the cook).

couch potato

someone who spends all their time watching television

Couch potato was first used as an American slang expression in the 1970s. It conjures up the image of someone slumped on a sofa or couch, with their shape or posture suggesting a potato. The origins of the phrase are much cleverer than simply an image, however, since it actually relies on a pun with the word 'tuber'. A potato is the tuber of a plant, while *boob tuber* was an earlier term for someone devoted to watching the *boob tube* or television ('boob' means 'silly person' and 'tube' comes from the cathode ray tube in television sets).

send someone to Coventry

refuse to associate with or speak to someone

This phrase goes back to the 1760s, but why *Coventry* should have been chosen to represent the worst destination possible isn't absolutely certain. It is most likely to be connected with the English Civil War (1642–49). The garrison of Parliamentarian soldiers stationed in Coventry was apparently deeply unpopular with the town's inhabitants, who refused to associate with them socially. Another explanation links it to the fact that as Coventry was a staunchly Parliamentarian city, many Royalist prisoners were sent there to be held in secure captivity.

crack of dawn

very early in the morning

This expression is only recorded from the late 19th century, with the earliest examples being in dialect and American use and in the form *crack of day*. The *crack* referred to is the instant of time taken by the crack of a whip. It seems likely that the phrase also has echoes of the earlier expressions *break of day* and *daybreak*, with the idea of the sky cracking or breaking open to reveal a sliver of light.

come a cropper
suffer a defeat or disaster

This phrase appears to have its origins in mid 19th-century hunting slang, where a *cropper* meant 'a heavy fall'. The word *cropper* itself probably came from *neck and crop*, a phrase meaning 'bodily' or 'completely' which is rarely heard nowadays. The meaning of *crop* in the phrase isn't precisely clear, but it probably means 'a crop of hair'.

cross your fingers
hope that your plans will be successful

This expression and the related *keep your fingers crossed* refer to the practice of putting one finger across another when hoping for good luck. Fingers are also sometimes crossed behind the back when telling a lie, to ward off any punishment that might be meted out for lying. The gesture in both cases is a scaled-down version of the Christian action of drawing the shape of a cross over the chest with the hand as a request for divine protection or blessing. This is also the source of the expression *cross my heart (and hope to die)*, the statement being made to emphasize the truthfulness of the statement being made, and sometimes reinforced by the tracing of a cross over the chest with the hand.

cross someone's palm with silver
pay someone for a favour or service

In former times, before a fortune teller would tell you what the future had in store, you had to trace the shape of a cross on the palm of their hand with a silver coin. The practice may have been seen as a confirmation of your belief in the truthfulness of what you were about to hear: a similar idea of sincerity is found in the phrase *cross my heart*.

cross the Rubicon
take an irrevocable step

The Rubicon was a small river in north-eastern Italy which in the 1st century BC marked the boundary between Italy and the Roman province of Cisalpine Gaul. In

49 BC Julius Caesar took his army across the Rubicon into Italy, and in so doing broke the law forbidding a general to lead an army out of his province. This act committed him to war against the Roman Senate and his rival general and statesman Pompey, a war in which he was finally victorious three years later. The current use of *crossing the Rubicon* goes back to the early 17th century.

off the cuff
without preparation

This expression dates from the 1930s and was first used in the US. The idea behind it is of a speaker relying only on notes written on their shirt cuffs to help them remember the main points of a speech, rather than reading out a prepared script. You might think that writing on fabric wouldn't be very effective, but in the early 20th century cuffs and collars were so stiffly starched that they resembled shiny cardboard, and were often detachable. These factors made writing on them particularly easy and it was common to have laundry notes and the owner's name marked on them.

a curate's egg
something that is partly good
and partly bad

The origins of this expression can be pinpointed precisely to a cartoon in an 1895 edition of the humorous magazine *Punch*. It shows a meek curate taking breakfast with his bishop, with the following caption: BISHOP: I'm afraid you've got a bad egg, Mr Jones. CURATE: Oh no, my Lord, I assure you! Parts of it are excellent!

The first recorded example of the phrase itself appeared a mere ten years later, in a publication entitled *Minister's Gazette of Fashion*: 'The past spring and summer season has seen much fluctuation. Like the curate's egg, it has been excellent in parts.'

curry *favour*
try to win favour with flattery and obsequious behaviour

This expression, dating from the early 16th century, has nothing to do with cooking or the Indian subcontinent. In fact it comes from the verb *curry*, meaning 'groom a horse with a coarse brush or comb', which came into English from Old French. The particular phrase *curry favour* was altered from the medieval form *curry favel. Favel* or *Fauvel* was the name of a chestnut horse in an early 14th-century French tale who became a symbol of cunning and deceit. The idea behind 'grooming Favel' was that of flattering him or behaving in an ingratiating way in order to keep him well disposed.

cut *and run*
depart hastily from an awkward or dangerous situation

This expression goes back to the early 18th century and the days of sailing ships. In an emergency, rather than hauling up the anchor in the usual, somewhat slow way sailors would be ordered simply to cut the anchor cable and set sail immediately. The word 'run' has been used of ships since Anglo-Saxon times, with the meaning 'sail straight and fast', but over time the nautical connection has been obscured by the more general sense of 'flee or escape'.

the **cut** *of someone's jib*
someone's appearance or look

This phrase, like the previous one, originates in nautical use. A *jib* is a triangular sail set forward of the mast on a sailing ship or boat. Although always triangular, it would vary greatly from being short and squat to tall and narrow. The characteristic shape and prominent position would make it a notable identifying feature of a ship, and this idea became extended to mean the impression given by someone's appearance or expression.

a damp squib

an event that is less impressive than expected

A squib is a type of small firework that burns with a hissing sound before it eventually explodes with a loud bang and a shower of sparks. If the explosive powder gets wet the firework won't explode very spectacularly, if at all.

a dark horse

a person who turns out to have unexpected talents

A *dark horse* was originally a horse that came first in a race it was not expected to win. The first example of the phrase seems to be in *The Young Duke*, a novel written by the 19th-century statesman Benjamin Disraeli: 'A dark horse, which had never been thought of . . . rushed past the grand stand in sweeping triumph.' However, it isn't entirely clear whether the horse in question here was simply a dark-coloured horse or one that was a surprising winner. *Dark* has long been used to mean 'secret or unknown', and the phrase clearly developed as a pun combining this idea with the sense of 'dark-coloured'.

go to Davy Jones's locker

be drowned at sea

Davy Jones's locker is a term for the bottom of the sea, especially when it is the last resting place of those drowned at sea. The earliest recorded use of the phrase is in Tobias Smollett's novel *The Adventures of Peregrine Pickle* (1751), where Davy Jones is described as 'the fiend that presides over all the evil spirits of the deep'. However, the exact origins of *Davy Jones* are far from certain and a range of explanations have been put forward. One suggestion is that the name *Davy* is a euphemism for the devil, because it contains the letters *d* and *v*. Another has *Jones* as an alteration of the name *Jonah*, recalling the tale of Jonah and the whale in the Bible. Colourful though these ideas may be, it is just as likely that the original *Davy Jones* was simply a pirate who drowned at sea: as with many phrases, we will never know the truth.

beat the living daylights out of someone

give someone a very severe beating

A person's *daylights* here are their vital organs, such as the heart, lungs, and liver, though originally the word referred to the eyes. *Having the daylights beaten out of you* implies a beating so violent that it would cause severe internal injuries. The word *living* is a later addition to the phrase, and rather a superfluous one as *daylights* already contain the sense of vital life force. Related expressions include *scare the living daylights out of someone*, meaning 'give someone a terrible fright'. The idea here is that the effect of extreme fear is as drastic as physical violence.

dead as a dodo

no longer effective or working

The dodo was a large, heavily built flightless bird found on the island of Mauritius in the Indian Ocean until it was hunted to extinction. The reason for its fate was apparently its lack of fear of human beings. When sailors and colonists came to the island in the 16th and 17th centuries they discovered that the unfortunate bird was very easy to catch and kill, a characteristic which gave it its name: *dodo* comes from Portuguese *duodo*, meaning 'simpleton'. By the end of the 17th century the dodo had died out. In *How to Become Extinct* (1941), the American writer and humorist Will Cuppy observed: 'The Dodo never had a chance. He seems to have been invented for the sole purpose of becoming extinct and that was all he was good for.' The bird's fate prompted the development of the expression *dead as a dodo*, which originally had the literal meaning 'completely dead or extinct' but which later was also used of anything no longer working or useful.

dead as a doornail
completely dead

Although this expression has been in use since the 14th century, we don't know for certain why doornails are particularly associated with death. A doornail was one of the large iron studs that were once used on doors to give additional strength or simply for the purposes of decoration. It has been suggested that a doornail was also the large stud struck by the knocker, which, being subject to constant pounding, could be considered well and truly dead. Support for this theory may come from another phrase, now no longer in use, namely *deaf as a doornail*: the idea might have been that the loud hammering from the doorknocker would cause the nail to go deaf.

a **dead** cat bounce
a brief, misleading sign of improvement in a deteriorating situation

This expression was first used by Wall Street traders in New York in the 1980s to describe a temporary recovery in share prices after a substantial fall. The rather tasteless idea behind it is that a dead cat dropped from a great height might well bounce when it hits the ground, but the fact that it bounces doesn't mean that it's alive after all. The choice of a cat as the object to be dropped is probably entirely arbitrary, but it may have been prompted by known cases of cats surviving falls from high buildings, or refer to the popular myth that cats have nine lives and so might appear to show signs of life after initially seeming dead.

the **deuce** of a —
used to emphasize how bad or difficult something is

The original meaning of *deuce* was 'a throw of two at dice'. Two is of course the worst or unluckiest throw you can have when playing with two dice, and *deuce* took on the additional meaning of 'bad luck or mischief'. By association it came to mean 'the devil', and was used in a number of expressions in which the words *deuce* and *devil* are interchangeable, for example *like the deuce*, meaning 'very fast', and *how the deuce . . .?*, meaning 'how on earth . . .?' Nowadays, these phrases suggest that the speaker is old-fashioned or upper-class, and so they tend to be found in fiction written or set some time in the past, as in this example from John Galsworthy's novel *The End of the Chapter* (1933): 'It seems there's the deuce of a fuss in the Bolivian papers.'

the devil to pay
serious trouble to be expected

This expression is generally thought to have arisen from the bargains supposedly made between wizards and the devil: in return for 'selling his soul', a wizard was promised extraordinary powers or wealth (see SELL YOUR SOUL, p. 152). A completely different explanation for the phrase, however, suggests that it is of nautical origin. The seam near a ship's keel is sometimes known as 'the devil' and because of its position it is very difficult to 'pay', or seal. This is the basis of an expanded version of the phrase *the devil to pay and no pitch hot* (pitch, or tar, would have been used to seal the seam).

play devil's advocate
express an opinion that you do not really hold in order to encourage debate

In the past, the *devil's advocate* was an official appointed by the Roman Catholic Church to challenge a proposed beatification of a dead person during a formal debate. He was so called because his job was to present everything known about the proposed saint, including any negative aspects, in order to make sure the case was examined from all sides. The term is a translation of Latin *advocatus diaboli* and the position was first established by Pope Sixtus V in 1587. It still exists today, but the official is now known as the *Promoter of the Faith*.

speak OR talk of the devil
said when a person appears just after being mentioned

This expression dates back to the mid 17th century and comes from the superstition that if you speak the devil's name aloud he will suddenly appear. The same idea is behind the phrase A NAME TO CONJURE WITH (p. 40).

dice with death
take serious risks

Dicing is playing or gambling with dice, and so the idea behind *dicing with death* is that you are playing a game of chance with death. The expression was first used by journalists in the 1940s to convey the risks taken by racing drivers in the pursuit of success in their sport, but it's now common in descriptions of any dangerous activity. It still seems to be very popular with journalists: 'Delivery driver Reg Crabtree has diced with death before but when he was trapped by six tonnes of frozen vegetables he thought he'd had his chips.' The phrase led to the use of *dicing* as a slang term among racing drivers for 'driving in a race', and is also the source of the adjective *dicey* meaning 'dangerous', first used by RAF pilots in the 1950s.

die hard

disappear or change very slowly

This expression is now generally used of habits or customs, but its origins lie in the grisly subject of public executions. It was originally used in the 1780s to describe criminals who died struggling to their last breath on the infamous Tyburn gallows in London. A few years later, during the Peninsular War (fought between France and Britain in Spain and Portugal from 1808 to 1814), Lieutenant-Colonel Sir William Inglis, commander of the 57th Regiment of Foot, lay severely wounded on the front line of the Battle of Albuera. He refused to be carried to safety, and urged his men to 'Die hard!' They followed his brave example, sustaining heavy loss of life, and all of the dead were found with their wounds on the front of their bodies. The battle was eventually won, and their heroism earned them the nickname 'the Die-hards'. In the early 20th century the name was taken up in political circles to describe those who were determinedly opposed to reform on certain issues, and the term *diehard* is still often used of someone who is stubbornly conservative or reactionary. It is also familiar as the title of the first of a trilogy of action movies starring Bruce Willis.

the **die** *is cast*

an event has happened or a decision has been taken that cannot be changed

The *die* in this phrase is a singular form of *dice*, now little used in Britain, but still current in North America (where you can throw one die). Although the first recorded example of the expresssion in English dates from the 1630s, its origins go back many centuries to the time of Julius Caesar. It is a translation of the words spoken by Caesar as he was about to take the momentous decision to cross the Rubicon river which marked the ancient boundary between Italy and Gaul. In doing this he was breaking the law which forbade a general to lead an army out of his own province, an act which led to a three-year war against the Roman Senate. In his account of Julius Caesar's life the Roman historian Suetonius reported the words as *iacta alea est*, 'the die is cast'.

go the **distance**
last for a long time

This expression has its roots in the world of boxing, although it is also used in other sports. A boxer who *goes the distance* manages to complete a fight without being knocked out, while a boxing match similarly described is one that lasts the scheduled length. In baseball, the phrase is used to mean 'pitch for the entire length of an inning', and in horse racing a horse that can *go the distance* can run the full length of a race without tiring.

lay something at someone's **door**
regard someone as responsible for something

One explanation of this phrase links it to a supposed old custom by which an unmarried mother would leave her baby on the doorstep of the man who was the father. This would identify him to the wider community and shame him into providing for the child.

like a **dose** of salts
very fast and efficiently

The salts referred to in this expression are Epsom salts, or crystals of magnesium sulphate. They have had a variety of medicinal uses since the 18th century, most notably as a very effective and fast-acting cure for constipation! The name *Epsom salts* comes from the town of Epsom in Surrey, where the crystals were first found.

drop a clanger

make an embarrassing mistake
or tactless remark

People have been *dropping clangers* since the 1940s, although the slightly less obtrusive *brick* has also been let slip since the 1920s. The idea behind dropping clangers and bricks is that both would make a very loud noise on hitting the ground and so draw immediate attention to the unfortunate individual responsible. *Drop the ball* is another expression that conveys the same idea: although it's used mainly in North American English, it's gaining in popularity on the other side of the Atlantic too. The meaning here is simply 'make a mistake' or 'mishandle things', with the idea of a sports player not keeping their eye on the ball and letting their concentration waver.

break your duck

score the first run of your
innings

The *duck* in this phrase is not the bird, but rather its egg, as it is a shortening of the term *duck's egg*, meaning a score of zero. If a batsman is 'out for a duck', they are dismissed without having scored a single run. The term arose from the shape of the figure 'o' being likened to the oval shape of a duck's egg. The cricketing expression dates back to the mid 19th century, but the same idea seems to occur a century earlier in racket sports. In these, the word *love* is used to mean 'a score of zero', and while some suggest that it comes from the phrase *play for love* (that is, play for the love of the game, rather than money), others connect the word with French *l'oeuf* meaning 'egg', again from the similarity in shape between an egg and a zero.

lame duck

an ineffectual or unsuccessful
person or thing

This expression was originally used among stock exchange traders in the mid 18th century to describe a person or company unable to pay their debts. The idea behind it may be that a lame duck could easily fall victim to a hunter or predator: in the case of a debtor, he would be at the mercy of his creditors. Since the mid 19th century *lame duck* has also been used to describe a politician or government in their final period of office, after their successor has been elected. In November 2000, following the election of his successor George W. Bush, Bill Clinton remarked: 'People say I will be a lame duck but I've got another ten weeks to quack', reminding the public that his term of office extended until January 2001.

dyed in the wool

unchanging in a belief or opinion

The basis of this phrase is the fact that yarn dyed in its raw state, before it is woven into a piece of fabric, has a much more even and permanent colour. The practice goes back many centuries of course, and the sense of 'unchanging' is also very old. Nowadays the expression is often used to refer to someone's political or sporting affiliation, as in the following example from *The Scotsman* newspaper: 'Voters and dyed-in-the-wool Tories are crying out for some "red meat" policies they can believe.'

your **ears** are burning

you have a feeling that someone is talking about you

The superstition that you experience a tingling or burning sensation in your ears when someone talks about you in your absence is an ancient one: the Roman scholar Pliny mentions it in his *Natural History*, for example, written in AD 77. Interestingly, the earliest written examples in English show that it was originally only your left ear that suffered. It was once believed that a tingling or burning left ear meant that a person was the subject of critical or malicious discussion, while a burning right ear meant that they were being praised.

early doors

early on in a game or competition

The origins of this phrase are to be found in the theatre. It goes back to the 1880s, when musical halls were a popular source of entertainment. If you were willing to pay a little extra you could gain admission to the theatre early on and have a better choice of seating. The period of admission covered by your ticket, known as *early doors*, ended a short while before the performance started. The practice died out in the 1950s but the phrase was resurrected in footballing circles in the 1970s in its current sense, with the legendary English manager Brian Clough providing the first recorded example. Speaking of his days at Derby County, he remarked: 'Early doors it was vital to me that they like me, too. But I became so attached to them as players that when I left Derby I found I liked them more than they liked me.'

eat crow

be humiliated by having to admit your defeat or mistake

This informal expression is used in North America, but there are similar phrases in British English, such as *eat dirt* and *eat humble pie*. The origin of the American version probably lies in the simple fact that the meat of a crow would be extremely unpalatable and would be eaten only as a last resort: early examples have *eat boiled crow* rather than just *eat crow*. It has been suggested that the phrase has its origins in a specific incident during the War of 1812 between the US and the UK, involving a confrontation between an American hunter and a British soldier. The soldier is said to have taken the the hunter's gun and ordered him to eat some of the crow he had just shot. Although the hunter obeyed, on regaining his gun he forced the British soldier to eat the remaining parts of the bird. It's a good story, but as the phrase isn't recorded until the 1850s, it's unlikely to be its true source.

The British equivalent *eat humble pie* is a mid 19th-century expression involving a pun on the word *umble*. *Umbles* were the internal organs and entrails of a deer: in early times these were often made into a cheap dish called *umble pie* (mentioned by the diarist Samuel Pepys in 1663). The pun comes from the idea of offal as an inferior food combined with the senses of *humble* meaning 'of low rank' and 'having a low opinion of your importance'.

economical with the truth

lying or deliberately withholding information

The idea of being economical with the truth can be traced back to Mark Twain's witty comment in *Following the Equator* (1897), an account of his travels round the world: 'Truth is the most valuable thing we have. Let us economize it.' The phrase itself developed in the early 20th century but did not gain widespread popularity until its use in 1986 during a government attempt to prevent the publication of *Spycatcher*, a book by a former MI5 officer, Peter Wright. Giving evidence at the trial, Robert Armstrong, head of the British Civil Service, reportedly said of a letter: 'It contains a misleading impression, not a lie. It was economical with the truth.' An Anglo-French version was coined by the British politician Alan Clark under cross-examination during another court case in 1992: 'Our old friend economical . . . with the actualité'.

effing *and blinding*

swearing

The *eff* in *effing* represents the spelling of the initial sound of the F- swear word: *eff* is also used as a substitute for the stronger word when a writer or speaker wants to avoid causing offence. Recorded examples of this euphemistic use go back to the 1940s, when it was unacceptable to use such terms in print. The *blinding* part of the phrase is probably from exclamations such as *blind me!* (the origin also of *blimey*).

one over the eight

slightly drunk

This British expression was first used by armed forces personnel in the 1920s. The explanation given in a slang dictionary written at the time is that a drinker should be able to manage eight glasses of beer without getting drunk: one more than eight and you might well be a bit tipsy. If a glass is a half pint, this is not such an unreasonable expectation, but if it's a pint then the soldiers and sailors of that time really did merit their reputation for having strong constitutions!

at the **end** *of your tether*

having no patience or energy left to cope with something

People have been describing themselves as *at the end of their tether* since the early 19th century, though those in North America tend to say that they're *at the end of their rope*. The image behind both expressions is that of an animal grazing on open ground. Animals such as horses are often tethered on a rope so that they can move where they like, but only within a certain range. When they reach the end of their tether—that is, when the rope is taut—they can go no further.

EATING AND DRINKING

The English language has concocted many idioms to do with eating and drinking, featuring a wide variety of foods ranging from the essential basics to the (debatably) less essential treats.

Basics

Bread is a staple part of many people's diet and this is reflected in a number of familiar phrases. It's often used as a metaphor for earning a living, as in the expression **take the bread out of people's mouths**, meaning 'deprive people of their living, especially unfairly'. Similarly, your **bread and butter** is your livelihood, or routine work that provides you with an income. When combined with 'bread', 'butter' can also convey an idea of luxury. Someone who **knows which side their bread is buttered on** knows what will benefit them, and if you are lucky enough to **have your bread buttered on both sides** you have a very easy, comfortable life.

Luxuries

Something that was even more of a treat than butter was jam. The phrase **jam tomorrow** describes a pleasant thing which is often promised but rarely materializes. It comes from Lewis Carroll's THROUGH THE LOOKING-GLASS (1871), in which the Red Queen tells Alice: 'The rule is jam tomorrow and jam yesterday—but never jam today.' Another popular tea-time treat is cake, and both **the cherry on the cake** and **the icing on the cake** signify a desirable feature that adds the finishing touch to something that is already very good.

Drink up!

The British are known for being a nation of tea drinkers, a fact reflected in the familiar phrase **not my cup of tea**, describing something that you don't like or aren't interested in. But we're not averse to a drop of something a bit stronger, such as beer. **Small beer** was originally a term for weak and watery beer, once drunk by both adults and children. The meaning was extended to refer to something unimportant or trivial, a sense that's first recorded in Shakespeare's OTHELLO. **Beer and skittles**, meaning 'fun or enjoyment', is usually used in the negative, to convey the gloomy perception that something is not in fact an endless round of enjoyment, as in 'married life isn't all beer and skittles.' More cheerful sentiments are expressed by the phrases **wine, women, and song** and **days of wine and roses**, evoking a carefree life of pleasure and entertainment.

The meat of the matter

Depending on your standard of living, meat used to be either an essential item of every meal or a rare luxury. The phrases **bring home the bacon**, meaning 'make money' or 'achieve success', and **save your bacon**, meaning 'save yourself from harm', both reflect the value of meat. In early use 'bacon' also referred to fresh pork, which was the meat most readily or cheaply available to the rural population. A type of meat that is rarely found on the menu nowadays is mutton, which features in the common expression **mutton dressed as lamb**, used in British English to describe an older woman dressed in clothes that are more appropriate for a much younger woman.

Seasoning

Salt has long been used for preserving and seasoning meat and is a very cheap commodity these days, but this wasn't always the case. Its former preciousness and high value are reflected in a couple of well-known expressions. If you describe someone as **the salt of the earth** you're saying that they are very kind, honest, or reliable. Similarly, a chef (for example) **worth his** (or **her**) **salt** produces a high standard of work and is well worth the salary they're being paid. Incidentally, the word 'salary' itself comes from Latin 'salarium' (from 'sal', meaning 'salt') and originally referred to a Roman soldier's allowance to buy salt!

push the **envelope**

approach or extend the limits of what is possible

This expression has nothing to do with bored office workers and piles of correspondence. In fact, it comes from the much more exciting world of aeronautics and aircraft design. In aeronautics, *envelope* is short for *flight envelope*, the set of limiting combinations of factors such as speed and altitude that are possible for a particular type of plane. During a flight, pilots who *push the envelope* are pushing the aircraft to or even beyond the current limits of performance. The phrase came into wider circulation after 1979 following its use in *The Right Stuff*, a novel by the American author Tom Wolfe about the early days of the American space programme, which was later made into an Oscar-nominated film. Nowadays, something seen as cutting-edge or extremely daring can be described as an *envelope-pusher* or as *envelope-pushing*.

an **even** break

a fair chance

Examples of this phrase are recorded from 1911, but it was popularized by the American comedian W. C. Fields around a decade later. He used it in his catchphrase, 'Never give a sucker an even break', which itself went on to become the title of one of his best-known films. Legend has it that Fields first used the catchphrase while performing on stage in the 1923 musical comedy *Poppy*, but it does not appear in the libretto for the play.

with an **eye** for the main chance

on the lookout for an opportunity to take advantage of a situation

The origins of this expression lie in the gambling game of hazard. Though involving only two dice, the game is quite complex, with the chances of a winning throw complicated by various apparently arbitrary rules. In the game, the person about to throw the dice calls out a number between five and nine. This number is called the *main* (originally also the *main chance*), and if they roll the main, or a number corresponding to it as specified in the rules, they've won. If they roll two ones, or a two and a one, they've lost. If they do neither of these things, then the number thrown is their 'chance' and they keep on throwing until either this comes up, in which case they're a winner, or the main comes up, and they're a loser. Rolling the main on the first throw is obviously the best chance of winning.

give someone the hairy eyeball

stare at someone coldly or contemptuously

This informal American expression has been used since the 1960s, and conjures up a very vivid picture. The image behind it is of someone glaring with their eyes narrowed and partly closed: the *hairy eyeball* is the effect of seeing the eyeball through the eylashes.

give your eye teeth for

do anything in order to have something

The *eye teeth* are the two pointed teeth in the upper jaw, so called because they are more or less immediately below the eyes. A clue as to why they might be regarded as particularly valuable is provided by their more usual name, canine teeth. The word 'canine' comes from the Latin term for a dog, and in dogs (and other meat-eating animals) these teeth are particularly distinctive. The canines in humans and other animals are used mainly for tearing off chunks of food, and so to lose them would indeed be quite a sacrifice to make.

fall OR land on your feet
be lucky in finding yourself in a good situation

The inspiration for this expression is a cat's ability to jump from a height and land safely on its feet without sustaining any injury. The first recorded use of the phrase is in *Barchester Towers* (1857), the second of the *Barchester Chronicle* series of novels by Anthony Trollope: 'It is well known that the family of the Slopes never starve: they always fall on their feet, like cats.'

take the fall
be blamed or punished, especially in place of the genuine culprit

Although this phrase is mainly used in North America, it is also familiar on this side of the Atlantic through imported detective fiction and television shows. The origins of the expression lie in the criminal underworld, and go back to the late 19th century. The word *fall* was first used among criminals to mean 'an arrest', and then later extended to 'a term of imprisonment': *taking the fall* meant that you were wrongly arrested or imprisoned for a crime committed by someone else. The term *fall guy*, meaning 'a scapegoat', developed from this expression in the early 20th century.

a false dawn
a misleadingly hopeful sign

Literally, a *false dawn* is a strange phenomenon most commonly seen in Eastern countries. Around an hour or so before the sun actually rises a faint light may be seen in the sky (the same phenomenon can also occasionally be seen in the evening sky to the west, after the sun has set). It is now more accurately termed *zodiacal light* because it is usually seen against the backdrop of the constellations of the zodiac and is known to be caused by the sun's light being reflected off the millions of particles of debris present in space.

play *fast* and *loose*
behave irresponsibly or immorally

Fast and loose was originally an old fairground gambling game in which the aim was to insert an object such as a stick into the loops of a twisted belt or rope so that it was firmly held in place. There are several ways of twisting a rope, and the person organizing the game would of course choose one that resulted in the stick slipping through. If the stick wasn't securely held, or made 'fast', the punter lost their money. This con trick has been around for centuries, and is mentioned in *The Gipsies Metamorphosed* (1621) by the poet and playwright Ben Jonson. The connection with the idea of being unfaithful and unreliable is just as old, and features in Shakespeare's play *King John*, in which King Philip asks rhetorically: 'Shall these hands . . . So newly joined in love . . . Play fast and loose with faith?'

a *ghost* OR *spectre* at the *feast*
someone or something that casts gloom over an otherwise pleasant occasion

This expression comes from a scene in Shakespeare's play *Macbeth*. The ghost of Banquo, who was murdered on Macbeth's orders, appears at Macbeth's banqueting table. He is invisible to everyone except Macbeth, and his presence is both a reminder of Macbeth's guilt and a warning that his attempt to hold power will ultimately fail. Another version of the phrase is *a skeleton at the feast*: this was probably inspired by the ancient Egyptian custom of having a coffin containing a carved and painted figure of the deceased present at the funeral banquet.

a *movable feast*
something which may appear or occur at varying times or dates

The literal meaning of *a movable feast* is a religious feast day that doesn't occur on the same calendar date each year. It is used in particular of Easter and the other Christian holy days whose dates are related to it. The term has been in use since medieval times, but the wider application is a relatively recent development, making its first appearance in the 1850s. In 1950 the American writer Ernest Hemingway observed: 'Happiness, as you know, is a movable feast.' He used the phrase as the title of a memoir of his life in Paris in the 1920s, which was published posthumously in 1964.

a *feather* in your cap
an achievement to be proud of

Early uses of this phrase suggest that having *a feather in your cap* marked you down as a foolish or unimportant person, although it is not clear why this should have been the case. Shakespeare embellished the idea in the following line from his play *Love's Labours Lost*: 'What plume of feathers is he that indited [i.e. wrote] this Letter?' Perhaps there was a feeling that having feathers in your headgear marked you out as a simple country person living at close quarters with chickens or other domestic fowl. However, by the mid 18th century the phrase had lost its negative implications and developed the positive meaning it has today. It may be that, as time moved on, the phrase became associated with exploits in battle rather than rural life: it was once the custom for knights to wear plumes on their helmets as a mark of their distinction or prowess in battle.

feet of clay
a fundamental flaw or weakness in someone otherwise greatly admired

The origins of this expression lie in a story told in the Bible in Daniel 2: 31–5. According to the prophet Daniel, Nebuchadnezzar, the king of Babylon, had a dream about a magnificent statue made almost entirely from different precious metals, all except for its feet, which were made partly of iron and partly of clay. In the dream a stone hits the statue's feet, shattering them and so causing the whole statue to collapse in pieces. Daniel interprets this to signify a future kingdom that will be 'partly strong and partly broken', and will eventually fall.

in fine fettle
in very good condition

Fettle was originally a Lancashire dialect word meaning 'dress, case, or condition', according to a glossary published around 1750. A century later the word had come into wider use, and although it was occasionally used in negative contexts or with words such as *good* or *high*, it is now almost always found in the expression *in fine fettle*. The word *fettle* itself comes from a verb which once had various senses, including 'prepare something' or 'groom an animal', but now only survives with the technical meaning 'trim or clean the edges of a piece of pottery before firing it', or the Northern English dialect sense 'make or repair something'.

fiddle while Rome burns

be concerned with trivial matters while ignoring the serious events going on around you

The source of this expression is the description of the behaviour of the Roman emperor Nero during the great fire that destroyed much of Rome in AD 64. According to the Roman biographer and historian Suetonius, Nero dressed up in his favourite stage costume, took up his lyre (not his fiddle: violins didn't appear until the 16th century!), and sang the whole of 'The Sack of Ilium' to celebrate the beauty of the flames. *Fiddle* was originally a standard term for playing the violin, and although this sense survives it's usually used either disparagingly or jokingly, or by violinists.

play second fiddle

be treated as less important than someone or something

The violins (informally called *fiddles*) of an orchestra are divided into two sections: generally speaking, the *first violins* play notes in a higher range than the *second violins*, and parts for the first violin usually have more of the main tune and are technically more difficult to play. This is the source of the idea that *playing second fiddle* involves a subordinate, less important role. In fact, the second violins' job is actually every bit as important and the music would lose a great deal without their supporting melodies and harmonies.

fifth column

a group within a country at war who are working for its enemies

Fifth column is a translation of the Spanish phrase *quinta columna* and originates from the Spanish Civil War (1936–9) between Nationalists and Republicans. As General Mola marched towards Madrid in 1936, leading four columns of Nationalist troops, he declared that he had a fifth column inside the city ready to assist in the attack. As it turned out, the Nationalists, under General Franco, did not succeeded in capturing Madrid until 1939.

not care OR *give a fig*

not have the slightest concern about something

Although this expression has been used in English over many centuries its exact origins are uncertain. It may have developed from the word *fig* meaning a type of fruit: this was also used to mean something worthless or contemptible, so *not care a fig* may contain the same idea as the expression *not care a scrap*. However, *fig* was also used from the late 16th century to describe a rude gesture made by putting the thumb between two fingers with the hand closed in a fist, or by flicking the thumb against the upper teeth. This gesture was particularly associated with Spain, being described in Shakespeare's *Henry V* as 'the fig of Spain', although the form itself seems to have come into English from the French phrase *faire la figue* (the Spanish equivalent is *dar la higa*). The idea that this sort of *fig* might be the source is reinforced by other, more recent expressions which follow the same pattern of *not give* or *care a —*, with various rude words substituted for *fig*.

finders keepers

used to assert that whoever finds something by chance is entitled to keep it

This phrase is a shortened version of *finders keepers, losers weepers*, and is typically used by children or jokingly by adults. Although it has only been recorded in English since the early 19th century, the idea itself is much older and even occurs in the works of the Roman comic dramatist Plautus, who was writing during the 2nd century BC. The earliest examples in English suggest that 200 years ago people were a little more sympathetic towards the unfortunate owner than they are today, as they say that losers are 'seekers', rather than 'weepers'.

be all fingers and thumbs

be clumsy or awkward in your actions

If you find yourself continually dropping things, you might well be described as *all fingers and thumbs*. If you'd been living in the 16th century, the phrase would have been *each finger is a thumb*, and in the 19th century *all thumbs*. Each of these expressions is actually rather puzzling when you look at how your hands work: the thumb is in fact the most mobile digit, and the one which gives human beings and other primates their manual dexterity and so is arguably the most useful! However, both make rather more sense than *all fingers and thumbs*, which is after all the normal human condition.

go through *fire* and water
face any peril

This is a very old expression, recorded as far back as the 9th century, and its origins lie in the legal processes of Ango-Saxon and medieval England. A person accused of certain crimes, especially witchcraft, would be put to trial 'by ordeal'. The word *ordeal* originally meant 'judgement', and the idea behind the method was that God would determine whether the person was guilty or innocent. The ordeal of fire involved either holding a red-hot iron bar or walking barefoot between red-hot iron ploughshares. If the person managed to come through this uninjured, they were deemed innocent (because God had protected them). The ordeal of water entailed two possibilities. In one, the accused had to plunge a hand into a pot of boiling water to retrieve a stone at the bottom; again, if they survived without burns, they were judged to be innocent. In the other method, used particularly for suspected witches, the person was tied up and thrown into a pond. If they sank, they were innocent (but, unfortunately, probably also dead by the time they were rescued). If they floated, they were guilty, because they had used their magic powers to stay on the surface of the water. All in all, it tended to be something of a no-win system, which sadly persisted well into the 17th century.

a *firm* hand
strict discipline or control

It might be thought that this expression refers to smacking or some other sort of corporal punishment, but in fact it originates from the world of horse riding. The phrase is a shortened version of *a firm hand on the reins*, and the idea behind it is that you need to keep a tight hold on the reins to prevent a lively horse from tossing its head about and refusing to go in the right direction.

of the *first* magnitude
the best or most considerable of its kind

The background to this phrase is the system used in astronomy to classify stars according to their brightness. The system was devised in the 2nd century BC by the Greek astronomer Hipparchus: under his scheme the brightest stars were the *first magnitude* and the faintest the *sixth magnitude*. In the 19th century the system was formalized according to a mathematical scale, and, because some stars are actually brighter than the first magnitude, also included zero and negative numbers. Nowadays, while the naked eye can only make out stars of the sixth magnitude, the most powerful telescopes can pick out ones of the twenty-fourth.

keep the *flag* flying
show continued commitment to something in the face of adversity

It used to be the practice in naval warfare for a ship to acknowledge defeat and show that it wished to surrender by lowering its flag. The idea of a ship continuing to fly the flag and battle on despite heavy bombardment readily came to stand for someone struggling on with a task in the face of extreme difficulty. The expression is also sometimes used of someone representing or supporting their country when abroad, in reference to a ship's flag identifying the ship's nationality.

a *flash* in the pan
a sudden but brief success

The origins of this expression are nothing to do with a spectacular failure in cooking, but in fact relate to old-fashioned firearms. An early type of gun was a flintlock, which had quite a complex firing mechanism. A small metal hollow or 'pan' located just above the trigger was filled with a quantity of gunpowder; on releasing the trigger, a flint would make a spark and thereby ignite the powder, which in turn ignited the main charge in the gun's barrel. Occasionally the main charge would fail to explode, so all that would happen was a flash of light and some smoke, while the shot stayed firmly lodged in the gun. From this we get the current sense of short-lived fame or success that fails to be sustained over the longer term.

flavour of the month
someone or something that is currently popular

We can thank a marketing push by the Illinois Association of Ice Cream Manufacturers back in 1946 for this particular expression. They devised an advertising campaign to run in a string of American ice-cream parlours in which a different flavour of ice cream would be singled out each month for special promotion. The campaign must have been successful as similar

continues on page 70

FOREIGN COUNTRIES

Perhaps because of its status as an island, Britain has always guarded its independence fiercely and regarded other countries with at best interest and curiosity and at worst suspicion or even hostility. These attitudes are often represented in the many familiar phrases featuring references to foreign shores.

Near but not dear

The 17th century was a time when England's relations with one of her closest neighbours, Holland, were at their most strained, with both England and Holland vying to become world leaders in terms of trade: no less than three wars were fought between 1652 and 1678. The enmity between the two was inevitably reflected in various insulting expressions. The Dutch had a reputation amongst the English for being hard drinkers, and so the phrase **Dutch courage** sprang up, used to describe an alcoholic drink that you quickly gulp down to bolster yourself before undertaking a daunting task. The Dutch were also believed to be rather miserly, a view surviving in the phrase **go Dutch**, meaning that you agree to share of the cost of a meal with someone. The expression only dates from the early 20th century, but the same idea is found in **Dutch treat**, first recorded in the 1880s.

Speak English!

The legendary reluctance of the British to learn a language other than English is apparently not a modern phenomenon. A number of foreign languages are used in phrases as typical examples of something completely unintelligible. The earliest is Greek, used in the remark 'it was Greek to me' made by Casca in Shakespeare's JULIUS CAESAR. The modern version **it's all Greek to me** is even more emphatic. Our Dutch neighbours are again targeted, in the expression **double Dutch**: the Dutch language was presumably regarded as impossible to understand, with 'double' being added to reinforce the idea of its incomprehensibility. The French don't escape a mention, although the meaning of the phrase **excuse my French** is rather different. It's usually added straight after a swearword, by way of an apology for the use of bad language. Those keen to maintain the entente cordiale might suggest the phrase reflects a self-deprecating awareness of a poor French accent, but sadly it's far more likely an indication that speaking French was regarded as no more acceptable than swearing.

Respect at last

Not all foreign parts are viewed with suspicion and superiority, although the passage of time seems essential to earning admiration. There has long been a high regard for classical civilizations, especially that of the Romans, and various phrases reflect this. The saying **all roads lead to Rome** expresses the view that there are many different ways of reaching the same goal. It goes back to medieval times and the works of Chaucer, and originates from the important position of ancient Rome as the centre of the Roman Empire. All the main roads of the empire converged at Rome, and later all the pilgrimage routes of medieval Europe too. The observation that **Rome wasn't built in a day** also alludes to the size of the Roman Empire, which extended over large parts of Europe, Asia, and Africa. It's been used to warn someone against rushing a complex or ambitious task since the mid 16th century.

promotions were going strong twenty years later in the ice-cream trade and the idea had also been adopted by other food retailers. By the 1970s the phrase was being used in its wider sense to describe anything (or anyone) currently at the height of their popularity. In 1996 *Cosmopolitan* observed: 'American sitcoms are the flavour of the month. British sitcoms—all lavatorial humour and canned laughter—have become the Pot Noodles of TV screen cuisine.'

a flea in your ear
a sharp reproof

The original meaning of *a flea in your ear* was 'something causing agitation or alarm', and this gives a better idea of the image behind the expression. It probably refers to the frantic scratching of dogs and cats when they suffer an infestation of fleas: having fleas in their ears would be particularly itchy and unpleasant. Nowadays people are usually *given a flea in their ear* or *sent away with a flea in their ear*, with the idea that a sound ticking-off will give them something to think about and hopefully cause some remorse, or at least some annoyance!

the flower of —
the finest individuals out of a number of people or things

Superficially, the image behind this expression is a fine display of flowers in full bloom, but this is a misunderstanding brought about by changes in English spelling. Originally the words *flower* and *flour* were the same, and the spellings were interchangeable until the 18th century. The expression *the flower of —* (as in 'the flower of English youth') uses a sense that in modern English would be spelled *flour*. The meaning of *flour* was formerly restricted to the finest quality of meal separated from the coarser parts by sieving, although today of course it simply means any powder made by grinding wheat.

with *flying* colours
with distinction

This phrase is typically used when talking about passing exams, but its origins are to be found on military battlefields. The *colours* were the regimental flag, and if they were still flying, or being displayed, at the end of a battle this indicated that the troops of that regiment were victorious; the conquered army usually had to lower its colours to signal surrender or defeat.

a *forlorn* hope
a faint remaining hope that is unlikely to be fulfilled

The expression *forlorn hope* comes from the Dutch *verloren hoop*, which literally means 'lost troop'. It originally referred to a group of soldiers chosen to lead the first attack of a battle, a mission which few were likely to survive. This military sense was established in the 16th century and persisted up to the 1870s, but the meaning we know today arose as early as the 17th century, as a result of a wrong (though understandable) misinterpretation of the two words by which *forlorn* was taken to mean 'hopeless' and *hope* to mean 'hope'. In fact, the English word *forlorn* and the Dutch word *verloren* are related but *hope* and *hoop* are quite different.

forty winks
a short sleep, especially during the day

A *wink*, now of course performed only by one eye, could formerly involve two—the word originally meant 'a brief closing of the eyes for sleep'. The same sense appears in *not sleep a wink*, and *not get a wink of sleep* shows a further development. The idea behind *forty winks* is that the sleep lasts the length of time taken by forty acts of closing and opening the eyes.

run the *gamut*
experience or display the complete range of something

The origins of this expression can be traced back to medieval music. *Gamut* was originally the name of the lowest note in the medieval scale, but the term also came to be applied to the whole range of notes used. In the 17th century it escaped from its musical context and came to mean the complete range of any particular thing: the American critic and humorist Dorothy Parker was being less than kind about Katharine Hepburn's acting skills when she remarked: 'She ran the whole gamut of emotions from A to B.'

run the *gauntlet*
go through an intimidating crowd or experience in order to reach a goal

The origins of this expression lie in an old military form of punishment recorded from the mid 17th century, in which a soldier found guilty of some offence was stripped to the waist and forced to run between two lines of men armed with sticks, who beat him as he went past. The practice clearly has nothing to do with gloves, and in fact the phrase originally used the word *gantlope*, which came from Swedish *gatlopp*, from *gata* 'lane' and *lopp* 'course'. *Run the gantlope* was first recorded in English in 1646: by 1676 *gauntlet* had begun to be used in place of *gantlope* because it was more familiar and had a similar pronunciation.

throw down the *gauntlet*
issue a challenge

Originally a *gauntlet* was specifically a glove worn as part of a medieval suit of armour. It was a custom in the Middle Ages for a knight to challenge another to a fight or duel by throwing down his gauntlet. If the other knight *took up the gauntlet*, it signified that he accepted the challenge. Nowadays challenges don't typically involve fighting and certainly don't require you to have a glove handy!

let the *genie* out of the bottle

set an unpredictable course of events in motion

A *genie* is a type of spirit in Arabian mythology. It can appear in various forms and can be either mischievous or well disposed towards humans. The genie usually inhabits a lamp or bottle until someone releases it to do some task by saying the necessary magic words or rubbing the container in a particular way. The most famous genie is the one who features in the tale of *Aladdin's Lamp* from the collection of stories known as the *The Arabian Nights* or *The Tales of One Thousand and One Nights*. Aladdin, the hero of the tale, finds an old lamp in a cave, which, when rubbed, summons a genie who grants the owner's wishes. This would seem to be a happy state of affairs, but genies could be rather hard to control, and the expression *let the genie out of the bottle* is generally used with the idea of impending disaster, while *putting a genie back in the bottle* is traditionally seen as an impossible task.

the *ghost* walks
money is available and salaries will be paid

This expression was first used in the 1830s by people working in the theatre. The popular explanation refers its origins to a production of Shakespeare's tragedy *Hamlet*, in which the ghost of Hamlet's father appears—or 'walks'—several times. Supposedly, on one occasion the actor playing the ghost refused to 'walk' again until the cast's wages, long overdue, were paid in full.

give up the *ghost*
(of a machine) stop working

The earliest use of *ghost*, recorded as far back as the 9th century, is in the sense 'a person's soul or spirit', and the original meaning of *give up the ghost* is 'die', the idea being that the soul is the source of life. This sense of *ghost* survives only in this expression, and in modern use the phrase often refers to equipment that has finally broken down beyond repair: 'The hailstones began to accumulate, obscuring the view of the road because the windscreen wipers of the hearse had long since given up the ghost, as it were.'

don't look a *gift* horse in the mouth
don't find fault with something you've been given

This old proverb goes back to the 16th century, but it can be found even earlier in a Latin version in the writings of St Jerome (5th century AD). A *gift horse* is literally a horse that has been given to you as a present, and the warning against looking in its mouth refers to one of the standard checks made by a prospective buyer of a horse. One way of determining a horse's age is by looking at its teeth, so buyers would often do this to make sure that it was no older than the seller claimed (see also LONG IN THE TOOTH, p. 106). Of course, if you were lucky enough to be given a horse, rather than having to buy it, it would be rather ungrateful of you to complain that you were getting an old nag! The phrase is often used today to advise someone to make the most of whatever opportunities come their way, even if they're not precisely what they were hoping for.

ginger group

a very active or radical group within a political party or movement

The origins of this term lie in a rather peculiar trick used by unscrupulous horse dealers from the late 18th century onwards. To make a worn-out animal look a bit more lively, the horse dealer would put a piece of ginger in its anus: as ginger is a fairly hot spice, friskiness was more or less guaranteed! This practice soon led to the development of the phrase *ginger someone up* meaning 'make someone more lively', and by the 1920s the term *ginger group* had also come into use.

gird up your loins

prepare yourself for future action

Gird is an old word meaning 'encircle a part of the body with a belt', and the expression *gird up your loins* might be thought to have something to do with putting on armour in preparation for battle. In fact, the phrase is of biblical origin and alludes to the long, loose garments typically worn in those times in the countries of the East. To allow greater freedom of movement, the robes would be hitched up and secured with a belt. There are several references to this practice in the Bible, for example in 1 Kings 18:46: 'Elijah . . . girded up his loins, and ran before Ahab to the entrance of Jezreel.'

little tin god

a pompous, self-important person

Tin has often been associated with inferior quality and cheapness, in contrast with other more precious metals, and this idea is the basis of this particular expression. It seems to have originated in *Plain Tales from the Hills* (1888) by the poet and writer Rudyard Kipling, who spent some of his life in India. He describes idols that he thinks are undeservedly revered: 'Pleasant it is for the Little Tin Gods When great Jove nods; But Little Tin Gods make their little mistakes In missing the hour when great Jove wakes.' The phrase tends to be used today to describe a self-important minor official.

kill the *goose* that lays the golden eggs
destroy a reliable and valuable source of income

This saying comes from the tale of the goose and the golden eggs, one of the famous fables of Aesop, a Greek storyteller of the 6th century BC. In the story, a man discovers an egg made of pure gold in the nest of one of his geese. Each morning he finds the goose has laid another golden egg, and soon he becomes very rich from selling the eggs. After a while, however, he grows dissatisfied with just one egg a day and kills the goose, thinking that he'll find a huge amount of gold inside her. Of course, he finds nothing at all, and with the goose dead has not even a single golden egg to look forward to. The American film producer Sam Goldwyn, famous for his colourful turns of phrase (or 'Goldwynisms'), once observed: 'That's the way with these directors, they're always biting the hand that lays the golden egg.'

your *gorge* rises
you are sickened or disgusted by something

In medieval times *gorge* was a term used in falconry for the pouch in a hawk's throat where food is stored for digestion (now called the 'crop') and it could also mean 'a meal for a hawk'. This gave rise to the more general meaning of 'the contents of the stomach', a sense which survives only in this expression. It's generally used to describe a physical response to something disgusting or nauseating: 'The pork smelt rancid and his gorge rose as he saw insects crawling out from under the rim.'

against the *grain*
contrary to your natural inclination

The *grain* referred to in this expression is the grain of a piece of wood, the way the fibres in the wood are arranged lengthwise. If you are sawing a piece of timber it is much easier to cut along the line of these fibres than across or against them.

grasp the nettle
tackle a problem boldly

This expression refers to the old belief that a nettle will only sting you if you touch it gently: if you grasp it firmly you won't suffer at all. The idea is enshrined in the following proverb: 'If you gently touch a nettle it'll sting you for your pains; grasp it like a lad of mettle, an' soft as silk remains.' While it seems unlikely, experience suggests that the belief is in fact true.

a *grey* area
an ill-defined situation which does not readily fit into an existing category

We often say that a matter 'is not black or white', meaning that it cannot be simply analysed or put into a single category. This is the idea behind using *grey* in this phrase, as grey is of course halfway between black and white. The expression was first used in the 1960s by town planners to describe urban areas that weren't quite in such a desperate state as slums but were in decline and in need of regeneration.

***grin* and bear it**
suffer pain or misfortune stoically

Originally, the feelings behind a *grin* were virtually the complete opposite of those prompting a broad smile. When it was first used in the 11th century *grin* meant 'an expression that showed the teeth' or 'a snarl', and it is the idea of lips drawn back in pain that is preserved in *grin and bear it*. It wasn't until the late 15th century that the word began to be used for various sorts of smile, from a forced, unnatural one, through a rather vacant, silly one, to the happy expression usually meant today. Nowadays, journalists describing antics involving nudity are fond of punning on the phrase, as this example demonstrates: 'GRIN AND BARE IT. Female politicians in Germany have tabled a motion calling for footballers to escape punishment when they take their tops off.'

in the *groove*
performing consistently well or confidently

The *groove* referred to in this expression is the spiral track cut in a gramophone record into which the stylus used to play it fits. *In the groove* was first used of jazz musicians and dates back to the 1930s, when jazz was starting to gain widespread popularity. The phrase is also the source of the word *groovy*, which initially had the same sense of 'playing or able to play jazz well' before developing the more familiar meaning 'fashionable and exciting'.

stick to your guns

refuse to compromise or change, despite criticism

The first uses of this expression refer to the battlefield, where *sticking to your guns* meant remaining steadfast in position, loading and firing a cannon despite being under constant bombardment. The phrase soon extended its meaning into the more general context of a refusal to alter an opinion or set of tactics: 'The congressional Republican leadership let loose with a barrage of criticism. Kerry stuck to his guns.'

give someone gyp

cause pain or discomfort to someone

The origins of the word *gyp* aren't certain, but it might be a dialect alteration of *gee-up*, an instruction to a horse to urge it to move faster. The idea behind this explanation is that the thing causing you pain or discomfort doesn't allow you to rest or relax. When you urge a horse on you may also dig your heels into its sides at the same time, and this could be compared to the sharp, intermittent pain felt in a part of the body that's *giving you gyp*.

H

hair *of the dog*

a small amount of alcoholic drink taken as a cure for a hangover

This expression is a shortened version of the phrase *a hair of the dog that bit you*. It comes from an old belief that someone bitten by a rabid dog could be cured of rabies by taking a potion containing some of the dog's hair. This belief stemmed from the idea that like cures like—that is, that a disease could be cured by a remedy connected to it. Interestingly, the same view forms the basis of homeopathy, a system of complementary medicine in which diseases are treated by administering tiny doses of natural substances that in larger amounts would actually produce symptoms of the disease from which the patient is suffering.

at **half** *cock*

when only partly ready

At half cock comes from the days of old-fashioned firearms: in its literal meaning it describes a flintlock pistol misfiring. The *cock* was the lever which was raised into position ready to be released when the trigger was pulled. A pistol which was *at half cock* had the lever raised halfway and held by the catch, which in theory ensured that it couldn't be fired even if the trigger was pulled. To fire the gun the lever needs to be *at full cock*, or fully raised. However, occasionally a pistol would be faulty and would go off early, at *half cock*, and this gave rise to the extended meaning of doing something before you're fully prepared for it.

Hamlet without the prince
an event taking place without the central figure

This origins of this expression can be traced back very precisely to an event reported in the *Morning Post* newspaper of 21 September 1775. According to the report, the actor who was to play Hamlet in a production of Shakespeare's play of the same name ran off with a local innkeeper's daughter just before the evening's performance. The finances of the theatrical company were perhaps in a rather precarious state, because the manager decided to go ahead anyway, merely informing the audience as the play was about to start that 'the part of Hamlet [was] to be left out, for that night'. In 1989 Michael Heseltine, who had resigned from the Tory Cabinet in 1986, made a particularly rousing speech at a Conservative Party conference, prompting the MP Robert Hughes to remark: 'A Conservative Cabinet without you is like Hamlet without the prince.'

make money hand over fist
make money very quickly

This is a phrase from the world of sailing, which originally had the form *hand over hand*. It described the action of a sailor climbing a rope or hauling it in, with each hand being brought over the other in rapid succession. By the 1820s the idea of speed had been extended to other contexts such as the rapid progress of a ship in pursuit of another, and soon after it was being used much more generally of any action done quickly. Nowadays it's almost always the making of money that is done *hand over fist*, but as well as making it you can now lose or spend it the same way. In 1994 an article in *Camping Magazine* commented: 'Euro Disney may be losing money hand over fist . . . but it's still fun.'

hang fire
delay taking action

As with *at half cock*, it was the complex firing mechanism of the old flintlock pistol which gave rise to this phrase. A small quantity of gunpowder would be loaded into a small metal hollow above the trigger; on releasing the trigger, a spark from a flint would ignite the gunpowder, and it in turn would ignite the main charge, causing it to explode and propel the shot out of the barrel. However, sometimes the powder in the pan would fail to explode immediately, perhaps because it was damp, and would merely smoulder. This of course would cause a delay in the firearm going off, and when this happened it was said to *hang fire*.

happy *as a sandboy*

extremely happy

Sandboys (who would also have been grown men as well as boys) have proverbially been described as 'happy' or 'jolly'—apparently because they were habitually drunk. A dictionary of slang terms published in 1823 defines a sandboy as an urchin selling sand in the streets, and explains that *jolly as a sandboy* referred to 'a merry fellow who has tasted a drop'. This association is reflected in a reference to a pub in Dickens's *The Old Curiosity Shop* (1840): 'The Jolly Sandboys was a small road-side inn . . . with a sign, representing three Sandboys increasing their jollity.' Sand was sold for use in building, for household chores such as cleaning pots and pans, and to spread on floors to soak up spillages, especially in pubs.

North Americans use the *clam* as their epitome of happiness, in the phrase *happy as a clam*. The longer version, *happy as a clam at highwater*, indicates the reason for the molluscs' good spirits. When the tide is high, the clams are covered by sea water and are able to feed to their hearts' content, without being exposed to predators.

happy *hunting ground*

a place where success or enjoyment is to be found

To some Native American peoples the *happy hunting ground* was an idyllic afterlife with plenty of game for hunting (the belief was not universal, and the 'heaven' of some other peoples, for example the Iroquois, required no hunting at all). In general use, the phrase now focuses on success or happiness found in a particular sphere of activity in this life. A 1993 edition of *Ideal Home* commented wryly: 'The recession has proved a happy hunting ground for many amateur decorators lured by the prospect of a cash-in-hand job.'

make a hash *of*

make a mess of

A *hash* is literally a dish of cooked meat cut into small pieces and then reheated in gravy. To some it may sound horribly typical of old-fashioned school dinners, but many distinguished writers have regarded it as a very tasty (and, of course, thrifty) meal. The earliest known example comes from a diary entry by Samuel Pepys in 1662: 'I had . . . at first course . . . a hash of rabbits and lamb.' However delicious it might have tasted, it probably didn't look very appetizing, and it wasn't long before the word developed the sense of 'a jumble of mismatched parts', forming the basis of the modern expression.

give someone their head

allow someone complete freedom of action

This expression comes from horse riding. Giving a horse its head meant allowing it to gallop freely rather than checking its pace by pulling on the reins. The idea of giving a horse freedom was readily extended to people, and the same image and meaning is to be found in the phrase *allow someone free rein*.

heart of oak

a courageous nature

This phrase has a nautical background and comes from the days of wooden sailing ships. The *heart* of an oak tree is the solid part running down the middle, which was traditionally used as timber for ships because of its great strength. The phrase *heart of oak* was popularized by the words of an 18th-century song: 'Heart of oak are our ships, Heart of oak are our men.' Other materials are also used with the word *heart* to symbolize certain human characteristics: for example, *gold* or *stone*. In 2000, the British racing driver Damon Hill remarked of his German rival Michael Schumacher: 'What you've got to remember about Michael is that under that cold professional Germanic exterior beats a heart of stone.'

*wear your **heart** on your sleeve*

make your feelings apparent

In the Middle Ages, when jousting was a popular form of entertainment, it was the custom for a knight to tie a favour from a lady to his sleeve. A favour was a ribbon, glove, or other small item belonging to the lady which she graciously bestowed on her chosen knight as a sign of her love or support. By wearing the gift on his sleeve he showed that he returned her feelings and probably also hoped that it would bring him luck in the forthcoming tournament. Despite the phrase's origins in the world of knights and armed combat, it has long been regarded as rather weak to show your feelings, a sentiment expressed by the former British prime minister Margaret Thatcher, not known for her sentimentality. In a television interview in 1987 she advised against it, saying: 'To wear your heart on your sleeve isn't a very good plan; you should wear it inside, where it functions best.'

heave in sight
come into view

Although this expression does come from the world of boats and sailing it has nothing to do with seasickness and heaving stomachs! The earliest senses of *heave* involve lifting or raising something with great effort, and from this developed the idea of something rising or rearing up. Sailors began to use the word to describe the way a ship would gradually come into view over the horizon, as if it was being hauled up by an invisible rope, and the meaning was soon extended to apply to anything which slowly appears in your field of vision.

be for the high jump
be about to be severely punished

This expression might conjure up pictures of shivering schoolchildren reluctantly lining up for various events on sports day, but (unless you really hated school sports) behind it lies a much grimmer scene. The phrase dates from the early 20th century, when it was a slang term used by soldiers to mean 'be put on trial before your commanding officer'. The image is actually of a person being executed by hanging, with the *jump* being the effect of the gallows trapdoor being suddenly opened beneath their feet.

high days and holidays

special occasions

In the calendar of the Christian Church there used to be two sorts of special day: a *high day* and a *holiday*. *Holiday* was originally spelled *holy day* and was a day set apart for religious observance. A *high day* was a much more important religious festival commemorating a particular sacred person or event. Today *holiday* has lost all its religious significance and is any day off from work or school, and so *holy day* is used if a specifically religious occasion is intended. With the Church's role being less influential in daily life, people are no longer as aware of the distinction between *high days* and *holidays*, and the phrase has crept into wider use to mean special occasions in general.

hit the ground running

start something new with energy and enthusiasm

The image behind this expression is of someone jumping down from a height, landing, and immediately setting off at a run. The earliest recorded example, dating from 1895, has a military setting; the phrase didn't reach the wider world until the 1960s. It became something of a cliché in the 1990s, typically associated with motivational 'management-speak'. Probably favoured because of its military associations, it conjured up images of soldiers disembarking rapidly from a helicopter and heading off on some daring SAS-style mission.

in hock

having been pawned

This phrase was first used in mid 19th-century American slang, where it meant 'in prison'. It comes from the Dutch word *hok*, meaning 'hutch' or 'prison'. The phrase soon developed the sense of 'in debt', probably from the way in which debtors were sometimes imprisoned until they could pay off their creditors. The sense of 'pawned' may have arisen from the image of an item locked away until the required sum was paid to retrieve it.

go the whole hog

do something completely or thoroughly

A number of explanations have been offered for this expression, which was first used in the United States in the early 19th century. The earliest examples are in a political context, prompting the idea that the phrase's origins might lie in the large political rallies which were then common in the US. At these rallies various ploys were used to woo potential voters, notably the provision of vast quantities of free food: a whole pig—or hog, in American English—was typically the favoured roast. Another idea is that the phrase comes from a fable about Muslims in *The Love of the World: Hypocrisy Detected* (1779) by William Cowper (an English poet who lived in retirement because of bouts of depression and mania—hardly an expert on Islam). According to this fable, certain Muslims, forbidden to eat pork by their religion but strongly tempted to have just a little, suggested that Muhammad had meant to ban only one particular part of the pig. They couldn't agree which part that was, and because 'for one piece they thought it hard From the whole hog to be debarred', between them they ate the whole animal, each one telling himself that his own portion didn't contain the part that was forbidden.

no **holds** barred
with no rules or restrictions

A *hold* is a particular way of grasping or restraining an opponent in wrestling and similar sports. The rules and regulations of each sport dictate what sort of holds are acceptable, and certain kinds, such as gripping your opponent round the throat, are classed as unlawful because they are too dangerous. Sometimes, however, *no-holds-barred* contests would be set up where participants were more or less allowed to do anything they liked. This wrestling terminology was adopted in a wider context to apply to any situation where the usual rules or conventional limits are ignored. The phrase is often used of interviews in which the interviewee gives surprisingly frank and explicit details about their personal life: in 1998, following her departure from the Spice Girls, 'Ginger Spice . . . agreed to a no-holds-barred interview with Jeremy Paxman on BBC2's hard-hitting *Newsnight*.'

an **honest** broker
an impartial mediator in a dispute

The first honest broker was the 19th-century German statesman Otto von Bismarck: the term was one of his nicknames. He more or less coined it himself in a speech in 1878, in which he likened the process of making peace to a business transaction, suggesting that what was needed was an honest broker (in German an *ehrlicher Makler*) who really wanted to make a deal. Bismarck had been the driving force behind unifying the numerous small German states in the mid 19th century, using far from peaceable methods and orchestrating wars with Denmark (1864), Austria (1866), and France (1870–1) to achieve this goal.

by **hook** or by crook
by any possible means

This is a very old expression, dating back to the 14th century, but its origins are uncertain. It most likely has a farming background, with the *crook* being a shepherd's hooked staff and the *hook* being a 'billhook', a type of heavy curved pruning knife. One indication as to how these implements might be used together comes from the writer and political reformer William Cobbett, who in 1822 described an ancient English forest law. According to this law, people living near a woodland were allowed to gather dead tree branches for fuel, using the *hook* to cut them off or the *crook* to pull them down.

hook, line, and sinker
said to emphasize that someone has been completely deceived

These three words refer to items used in angling: all form parts of a fishing rod, with the possibly unfamiliar term *sinker* being a weight used to sink the fishing line in the water. The image behind the expression is of a hungry fish deceived by the bait into gulping everything down.

off the **hook**
no longer in trouble

This is another expression from angling, like *hook, line, and sinker*, of which it is almost the opposite. The image here is of a fish managing to wriggle off the hook that lodged in its mouth when it took the bait: being 'on the hook' is a bad situation for the fish, but if it manages to get *off the hook* it is out of trouble.

on the **horns** of a dilemma

faced with a decision involving equally unpleasant alternatives

When the word *dilemma* first came into use in the early 16th century, it was a term used in the deeply complex subject of logic. It identified a form of argument that forces an opponent to choose either of two unfavourable alternatives. These alternatives were traditionally called 'horns' (translating the term used in Latin, the international language of European scholars at the time). Avoiding one 'horn' would result in the debater being impaled on the other, and they would always lose the argument.

horses for courses

different people are suited to different things

Not surprisingly, this phrase comes from the sport of horse racing. It's based on the idea that each racehorse is suited to one particular racecourse and will do better on that than on any other. This view among the racing fraternity was soon taken up by the wider public to mean that just because something suits one person, this doesn't mean that it will necessarily suit another.

straight from the horse's mouth

from the person directly concerned

This expression seems to have been first used by P. G. Wodehouse in the *Strand Magazine* in 1928: 'The prospect of getting the true facts—straight, as it were, from the horse's mouth—held him . . . fascinated.' Presumably the underlying idea is that the best way to get racing tips is to ask a horse directly!

a *hostage to fortune*

an undertaking or remark seen as unwise because it invites trouble

The word *fortune* here means 'fate', with the idea being that future events are no longer under a person's control but are in the hands of fate. The first recorded *hostages to fortune* were a man's family. The English philosopher Francis Bacon used the expression in an essay on the subject of marriage, written in 1625: 'He that hath wife and children, hath given hostages to fortune; for they are impediments to great enterprises, either of virtue, or of mischief.' Bacon clearly takes a rather dim, if not bitter view of marriage, as he goes on to say: 'Certainly the best works, and of the greatest merit for the public, have proceeded from the unmarried or childless men.' We don't know much about Bacon's life with his wife Alice Barnham, thirty-four years his junior, but the fact that various contemporary sources suggest that he was homosexual may explain his rather jaundiced attitude.

I

the tip of the iceberg

the small visible part of a much larger problem that remains hidden

This expression is surprisingly recent, being recorded only from the 1960s, but the deceptive appearance of *icebergs* has been familiar to voyagers for much longer, most famously to the unfortunate passengers on SS *Titanic*, which sank after colliding with an iceberg in the Atlantic on 14 April 1912. Following his resignation as Chancellor of the Exchequer in 1989, Nigel Lawson described an article by Margaret Thatcher's economic advisor, Alan Walters, as 'the tip of a singularly ill-concealed iceberg, with all the destructive potential that icebergs possess'.

have had a good innings

have had a long and fulfilling life or career

This phrase comes from cricket, a sport that has long been popular in England and other parts of the world, although some of its rules and laws make it a bit of a mystery to outsiders. The origins of this particular expression are fairly straightforward, however: an *innings* is the period during which one side or batsman has a turn at batting, and a *good innings* is one during which a lot of runs are scored. The first example of the word's extended meaning is in Charles Dickens's *The Pickwick Papers* (1836), where it means someone's turn or opportunity to do something: 'It's my innings now, gov'rnor, and as soon as I catches hold o' this here Trotter, I'll have a good 'un.'

the Iron Curtain

a barrier regarded as separating the former Soviet bloc and the West

This phrase has long been particularly associated with a speech made by Winston Churchill in March 1946, in which he observed that 'an iron curtain has descended across the Continent [of Europe]'. However, the phrase had been used in reference to the Soviet Union in the 1920s, and in fact had the more general meaning of 'an impenetrable barrier' as far back as the early 19th century. Its origins actually lie in the world of the theatre. Today's theatres employ a flame-resistant safety device called a *fire curtain*: in the late 18th century the protective screen would have been made of iron, a literal *iron curtain*.

have many irons in the fire

have a range of options or commitments

There are many different tools and implements described as *irons* because they are or were originally made of iron, for example *branding irons* and *fire irons*. This particular expression, which has been in use since the 1540s, comes from the way such tools are made. A blacksmith has to heat the iron objects in a fire until they reach the critical temperature at which they can be shaped. If they have several items in the forge at the same time, they can remove one and hammer it until it has cooled and is no longer malleable, then return it to the fire to heat up again and work on another one in the meantime.

strike while the iron is hot

make use of an opportunity immediately

This expression dates back to the Middle Ages and was first used by Chaucer. Like the previous phrase, it comes from the work of a blacksmith. A blacksmith works with wrought iron, which can only be hammered into shape when it is red hot: if it isn't yet hot enough or has cooled down too much, it won't be sufficiently malleable. So someone advised to *strike while the iron is hot* is being warned that the opportunity to do something may only be available for a short time.

hit the jackpot

have great or unexpected success, especially by making a lot of money quickly

Jackpot was originally a term used in American English in the card game poker. In a particular form of the game, known as *draw poker*, each player had to keep adding to the pool (or pot) of potential winnings until someone had a pair of jacks or higher cards. Soon *jackpot* was being used for any large money prize that accumulates until it is won, as in a lottery or a fruit machine, and the link with cards was forgotten. The meaning of 'make money quickly' is first recorded in the 1940s, but before this another extended use was current among the criminal fraternity. In the early 20th century it was a slang expression for a difficult or awkward situation: quite the opposite of how most of us would regard winning a lottery jackpot!

a Jekyll and Hyde

someone who alternately displays good and evil personalities

The first *Jekyll and Hyde* are found in Robert Louis Stevenson's novel *The Strange Case of Dr Jekyll and Mr Hyde* (1886). Dr Jekyll, a hard-working, philanthropic man, pursues the idea that both good and evil lie in all people, and develops a drug which creates a separate personality, manifesting in the character of Mr Hyde, into which he can channel all his evil impulses. At first he can become Mr Hyde at will, but gradually his evil persona takes control of him. The extended use appeared within two years of the book's publication, and was further popularized by a silent film made in 1920 and a talking version (the first of many) made in 1931.

a joker in the pack

a person or factor likely to have an unpredictable effect on events

In a pack of playing cards, a *joker* is an extra card that doesn't belong to any of the four suits of clubs, diamonds, hearts, and spades. It usually has a picture of a jester printed on it and is used as a wild card in various games. If you have a joker in your set of cards, you can totally confound your opponents' calculations of what you hold and play an unexpected winning hand.

keep up with the Joneses

try to do as well as or better than your neighbours

Jones is a very common British surname and has been used to represent a person's neighbours or social equals since the 1870s. However, the first occurrence of this particular expression was in the title of an American comic strip in the New York *Globe* newspaper in 1913: 'Keeping up with the Joneses—by Pop'. 'Pop' was the cartoonist Arthur R. Momand, and the strip was based on his own experiences. As newly-weds, he and his wife moved into a smart area of New York that was in reality beyond their means, but nonetheless they tried to emulate the lifestyle of their wealthy neighbours; eventually they gave up and relocated to a more modest apartment in New York City. Momand's depiction of these early days proved very successful and the comic strip ran in American newspapers for many years.

jump the shark

(of a television series) reach a point when far-fetched events are included merely for the sake of novelty

This expression arose in the 1990s to describe the all-too-familiar situation when a long-running television series becomes so stale that ludicrous events are incorporated into the storyline to try to shore up dwindling ratings. Of course the phenomenon is much older than the phrase, but the particular event that gave rise to its use occurred in the American series *Happy Days*: in one episode towards the end of its run the central character, the Fonz, literally jumps over a shark while waterskiing. Although the expression features mainly in television reviews, it has also been extended to describe any situation where desperate measures are taken in response to a decline in quality.

a pretty OR _fine_ _kettle_ _of fish_

an awkward or muddled state of affairs

It's rather hard to picture how you might fit a fish into the modern container used for boiling water for a cup of tea, but originally a _kettle_ was any container used to heat liquid over a fire. This original meaning can be seen in _fish kettle_, the term for a long, thin, deep pan specifically designed for cooking whole fish. Unfortunately, this explanation alone doesn't shed much light on the origin of the popular phrase, which is first recorded in the 1740s. A travel book from the 1790s may provide a clue when it describes a _kettle of fish_ as a term used in Berwick-upon-Tweed for a high-society picnic where freshly caught salmon were cooked in kettles on the banks of the River Tweed. Perhaps the phrase came about because the presentation of the cooked fish fell rather short of the standards the guests were used to,

given the familiar difficulties of cooking outdoors for large numbers. An alternative suggestion links the phrase to Canadian English and the fishing industry. A *quintal of fish* is an old measure equivalent to a hundredweight of fish, but Newfoundland English used the word *kentle* instead, which sounds rather like *kettle*. This idea may seem plausible, especially in relation to the similar phrase *a different kettle of fish*, meaning 'a completely different matter or type of person', but all the evidence indicates that both expressions were in fact British in origin.

kick against the pricks

hurt yourself by continuing to resist something that cannot be changed

The source of this phrase is the account in the Bible of Saul of Tarsus's experiences on the road to Damascus. Saul was an opponent of the followers of Jesus and was on his way to Damascus to arrest any Christians in the city. En route, he had a vision and heard the question: 'Saul, Saul, why persecutest thou me?' When he asked who the speaker was, he was told: 'I am Jesus whom thou persecutest: it is hard for thee to kick against the pricks.' After seeing the vision Saul was temporarily struck blind; on recovering his sight he became a Christian convert. Under a new name, Paul, he later became one of the first major Christian missionaries and theologians. The image behind the phrase itself is that of an ox fruitlessly kicking out at a spur or goad: the more it kicks, the more the driver goads or spurs it.

kick the bucket

die

This informal expression has been in use since at least the late 18th century, but its exact origins remain rather unclear. One suggestion is that the *bucket* is one used to stand on by someone committing suicide by hanging themselves, the person first standing on it and then kicking it away. Another idea associates it with an old sense of *bucket* meaning 'a beam used for hanging something on'. This meaning was also found in Norfolk dialect, in which it specifically referred to a beam from which a pig about to be slaughtered was suspended by its heels. Both explanations evoke the rather gruesome image of a person or animal struggling in the throes of death.

kick over the traces

refuse to accept discipline or control

The *traces* in this expression are the two side straps by which a draught horse is attached to the vehicle it is pulling. If the animal is rather uncooperative or skittish and kicks out over these straps, the driver would have difficulty trying to regain control of it: more than likely a crash would result, causing injury or death to both man and beast.

a **king's** ransom

a huge amount of money

This expression is first recorded in Christopher Marlowe's play *Doctor Faustus* (1590): 'I'll not speak another word for a king's ransom'. However, its literal meaning goes back to feudal times. In the Middle Ages prisoners of war could be freed on payment of a ransom. The ransom varied according to the rank of the prisoner, and so a king, as holder of the highest rank, would require a vast sum of money to be paid in order to secure his release.

the **kiss** of death

an action or event causing certain failure for an enterprise

Although this phrase is relatively recent, with examples dating back only to the 1940s, it is thought to refer to an episode in the Bible. According to the biblical account, Judas Iscariot identified Jesus to soldiers out to arrest him by greeting him with a kiss. The expression is often used of apparently beneficial or well-meaning actions which somehow tempt fate and have the opposite result to that intended, as in the following example from *The Guardian*: 'Let us hope that the critics' approval does not, at the box office, prove a kiss of death.'

knock something on the head

put an end to an idea or plan

The purpose of literally knocking a person or animal on the head is of course to kill or stun them. The phrase began to be applied in abstract contexts as long ago as the 16th century: the *Oxford English Dictionary* records an example from 1584 in which 'witchcraft . . . is knocked on the head'. Nowadays the phrase often refers to dismissing a rumour or theory once and for all: 'The Micromega Microline system . . . knocks on the head the myth that hi-fi needs to be big and macho to sound any good.'

knock *spots off*

outdo someone or something easily

The origins of this expression are thought to lie in the world of competitive shooting. Contestants keen to show off their skilled marksmanship would be required to shoot out the pips or spots on a playing card. The person shooting out the most would, of course, be the winner, and might well have been described as *knocking spots off* their rivals. The expression originated in the United States, but it's now found mainly in British English. In 1997 the *Sunday Times* observed: 'Dino Baggio is a very good player . . . but [Paul] Gascoigne could knock spots off him, technically.'

at a rate of **knots**

very fast

A *knot* is a measure of speed, equivalent to one nautical mile an hour and used especially with reference to ships, aircraft, or winds. This particular expression gives a clue as to how the word *knot* was adopted as a nautical unit of speed. A line with knots tied at fixed intervals and a float on the end was wound on to a reel, and the length run out over a certain time would be used to gauge the ship's speed. If the line unwound very rapidly, with each knot appearing in quick succession, then the ship might be said to be going *at a rate of knots*. The phrase is now used of anything travelling (or happening) at great speed: 'Fixed-rate mortgages are rising at a rate of knots and discounted-rate deals now look much cheaper.'

ladies who lunch

women who meet for lunch in expensive restaurants

The source of this expression is the title of a 1970s song by Stephen Sondheim, in which he pokes fun at certain members of the affluent charity fund-raising set: 'Here's to the ladies who lunch— Everybody laugh. Lounging in their caftans and planning a brunch On their own behalf.' Early on the phrase reflected the song's original meaning and was used of rich American women organizing fashionable charity lunches. Since the 1990s, however, examples tend simply to describe rather disparagingly (and, possibly, enviously!) women with plenty of money and leisure time: 'As if Notting Hill's ladies who lunch were not already spoilt for choice when it comes to exclusive shopping experiences!'

the Old Lady of Threadneedle Street

the Bank of England

The Bank of England is located on Threadneedle Street in London, but this particular nickname comes from the caption to a cartoon by James Gillray published on 22 May 1797. The cartoon shows an old lady wearing a dress made of one-pound notes who is seated on a strongbox of gold, trying to fend off the amorous advances of the prime minister of the time, William Pitt the Younger. The caption reads 'Political Ravishment, or The Old Lady of Threadneedle Street in Danger'. Pitt's government had made repeated demands on the Bank of England to pay for wars against France, and the consequent fall in its reserves had led to the first ever issue of one-pound notes. The phrase is often shortened to simply *the Old Lady*, as in this example from the money page of the *Daily Telegraph*: 'The consumer may take some time to heed the Old Lady's warnings, but we usually listen in the end.'

the **land** of Nod

sleep

This expression was first used by the satirist Jonathan Swift in *Polite Conversation* (1731–8), and is a pun combining the idea of 'nodding off', or going to sleep, and a rather darker biblical reference. The land of *Nod* was the place to which Cain was banished for murdering his brother Abel (Genesis 4:16), a place which now tends to be described as *the land God gave to Cain*, since *land of Nod* no longer sounds unpleasant enough. Incidentally, John Steinbeck took the title of his best-selling novel *East of Eden* (1952) (made into a classic film starring James Dean in 1955) from the same verse of the Bible: 'And Cain went out from the presence of the Lord, and dwelt in the land of Nod, on the east of Eden.'

in the **lap** of the gods

(of the success of a plan or event) outside your control

This expression can be traced back to several passages in the works of the Greek epic poet Homer, thought to have been written during the 8th century BC. The idea is that the course of events is determined by the gods, and so is completely outside human control. The phrase probably comes from the image of someone trying to placate or influence a person in authority by placing gifts in their lap as they sit ready to pass judgement.

rest on your laurels

make no further effort as you are satisfied with what you've already done

Laurel in this expression refers to the shrub which is now commonly called a *bay tree*, or sometimes *bay laurel*. The phrase goes back to ancient Greek times, when a wreath made of bay leaves was awarded to someone who had achieved something particularly noteworthy, especially the winner of an event in the Pythian Games held at Delphi. At the 2004 Olympic Games in Athens this tradition was revived, with medal-winners also being given a laurel wreath to wear during the victory ceremony.

lay a ghost
dispel a distressing or worrying thought

The literal meaning of *lay a ghost* is 'exorcize an unquiet or evil spirit'. The practice is centuries old: *lay* in this sense is first recorded in Shakespeare's play *Romeo and Juliet*. The phrase may have arisen from *lay someone to rest*, meaning 'bury a body in a grave', the idea being that the ghost cannot rest because it has outstanding issues to address with the living. Surprisingly, however, the current sense of the phrase—in which being beset by a persistent worry or problem is equated with being haunted by a malevolent ghost—is not recorded until the mid 19th century, in Tennyson's poem *In Memoriam*: 'He faced the spectres of the mind And laid them.'

turn over a new leaf
improve your behaviour or performance

The *leaf* in this expression is a page of a book, not a part of a plant or tree. Today, if you *turn over a new leaf* it always means you are making a change for the better, but previously you might simply have been making any change in your behaviour, even showing a change for the worse.

spring a leak
develop a leak

Nowadays we talk about all sorts of things *springing a leak*, from hoses to washing machines, but the first examples of the phrase, dating back to the early 17th century, only refer to ships. The word *spring* described the way the timbers of a wooden sailing ship sprang out of position as a result of some sort of collision and so started letting in water.

as large as life
(of a person) conspicuously present

This expression goes back to the days before photography when portrait painting was very common, being almost the only way of capturing a person's likeness. Professional artists did not, of course, come cheap and a good way of showing off your wealth would be to have a portrait painted which was life-size. Early versions of the expression, dating from the mid 17th century, are *greater than* or *bigger than the life*, with the modern form first recorded in the early 19th century.

The metaphorical use, sometimes expanded to *as large as life and twice as natural*, is attributed to the Canadian humorist T. C. Haliburton (1796–1865) but was probably popularized by Lewis Carroll's *Through the Looking Glass* (1871). The King's messenger, Haigha, explains to the Unicorn that Alice is a child, going on to say: 'We only found it to-day. It's as large as life, and twice as natural!'

light the blue touchpaper
do something that creates a tense or exciting situation

A *touchpaper* is a type of fuse consisting of a twist of paper impregnated with saltpetre, or potassium nitrate, to make it burn slowly. It's now only used with fireworks, but in the past would also have been a means for igniting gunpowder. Obviously, once the touchpaper has been lit there are some anxious moments as it slowly burns towards the powder and everyone waits for the deafening explosion and pyrotechnics. The expression is often used after saying something deliberately provocative or inflammatory: in such cases people are likely to *light the blue touchpaper and retire* to a position of safety!

out on a limb
without support from anyone

The *limb* in this expression is the branch of a tree, and the image conjured up is of someone clinging precariously to the end of a projecting branch, with nothing or no one to assist them in their difficult situation. People are often said to *go out on a limb*, meaning 'take a risk' or 'act boldly', as in: 'It's just a theory but I wouldn't go out on a limb like this if I didn't feel we had the data to support it.'

the bottom line

the fundamental and most important factor

The *bottom line* is actually a term used by accountants with a literal meaning 'the final total in a profit-and-loss account'. The most important issue for a business is, of course, whether it is making or losing money, and this idea gave rise to the extended meaning. It was first recorded in American English in the 1960s, before becoming popular on the other side of the Atlantic too. It's now used in a wide range of contexts—this example comes from the magazine *Elle*: 'The bottom line is clear: by a woman's mid-thirties, age makes getting pregnant more difficult.'

enter the lists

issue or accept a challenge

The origins of this expression have nothing to do with signing up for some risky undertaking, but in fact go back to the days of knights and jousting tournaments. In medieval times the *lists* were the enclosed area (also known as a *tilt yard*) where jousts and tilting matches took place. The *lists* were actually the barriers surrounding this area, but the meaning was extended to refer to the yard itself. If you *entered the lists* you were formally agreeing to take part in combat.

use your loaf

use your common sense

Loaf in this informal British expression most probably comes from the rhyming slang phrase *loaf of bread* meaning 'head'. It is first recorded in a 1920s dictionary of army and navy slang as '*Loaf*, head, e.g., Duck your loaf, i.e., keep your head below the parapet'. The instruction *use your loaf* itself is known from the 1930s.

lock, stock, and barrel

including everything

The *lock*, *stock*, and *barrel* are all parts of an old-fashioned firearm: only the stock and barrel are found in modern guns. The lock was the mechanism for exploding the charge; the stock is the part to which the firing mechanism and barrel are attached, held against your shoulder; and the barrel is the cylindrical tube out of which the shot or

continues on page 106

LEGENDS AND MYTHS

Myths describe the early stages of the world according to the beliefs of ancient civilizations and contain vivid depictions of the exploits of gods and heroes. The many Greek and Roman legends that have been read and studied over the centuries have proved a fruitful source for English phrases.

Heroes and villains

Legendary heroes feature prominently. Hercules was a man of superhuman strength who had to perform twelve immense tasks or labours as a penance for killing his children in a fit of madness. We now use the phrases **a labour of Hercules** and **a Herculean task** to describe something requiring enormous strength or effort. However, no matter how hard you try to do something, your **Achilles heel**, or your only weakness or vulnerable spot, might still let you down. When the hero Achilles was a baby, his mother, the nymph Thetis, dipped him into the river Styx in order to make him immune to any injury or harm. She had to grasp him by one of his heels to do this, but of course this meant the water didn't touch that part of him. Achilles later became a hero of the Trojan War but was finally killed by an arrow striking him in his only vulnerable spot: his heel.

The Trojan War is the source of two other well-known expressions. One of the most common uses of **a Trojan horse** nowadays is the computing sense all too familiar to Internet users, meaning 'a program that breaches the security of a computer system', but earlier in its history it described a person or thing intended to secretly overthrow an enemy. The original Trojan horse was a huge hollow wooden statue of a horse in which the Greeks are said to have concealed themselves in order to secretly enter and capture the city of Troy. This trick was also the origin of the saying **beware of Greeks bearing gifts**, meaning 'be suspicious of the motives of rivals or enemies showing apparent generosity or kindness'.

Fabulous creatures

Many other mythological beings and beasts are represented in English phrases. Sirens were a type of sea nymph or winged creature whose beautiful singing lured unwary sailors on to the rocks. They have given us the phrase **a siren call**, used to describe the appeal of something alluring but dangerous. If their singing sounded anything like a modern siren's wail, however, most sailors should have been able to resist the lure fairly easily! Another danger to deal with was Cerberus, a three-headed dog who guarded the entrance to the underworld. The Trojan warrior Aeneas managed to get past him by giving him a drugged cake, or a 'sop'. This image is the basis for the idiom **a sop to Cerberus**, meaning 'something offered by way of appeasement'.

J. K. Rowling's Harry Potter had a similar encounter in HARRY POTTER AND THE PHILOSOPHER'S STONE, although in his case the dog was called Fluffy and only had to be sent to sleep by some music! Later, Harry also meets the phoenix, a fabled bird resembling an eagle. The tale of the phoenix is the source of the phrase **rise from the ashes**, meaning 'be renewed after destruction'. According to ancient Egyptian legend, only a single phoenix was alive at any one time and each lived for around five or six centuries. At the end of this period it would burn itself on a funeral pyre ignited by the sun and fanned by its own wings and then be born again from the ashes to live again for another five hundred years or so. Phoenix, the capital city of the American state of Arizona, is named after this legend as it was founded on the ancient ruins of a Native American settlement.

bullet is fired. The expression first appears in the early 19th century in the alternative version *stock, lock, and barrel*, used by the novelist Sir Walter Scott in a letter written in 1817. This version was the more common in the 19th century, but the modern one took over in the early 20th century. A vivid expansion of the phrase was used as the title of the 1998 British gangster film *Lock, Stock, and Two Smoking Barrels*.

at loggerheads
in violent dispute or disagreement

The origins of this expression are rather obscure. The earliest meanings of *loggerhead*, dating from the late 16th century, were 'a disproportionately large head' and 'a stupid person' (similar to the current *blockhead*). Around half a century later the word was applied to various animals with very large heads, notably the *loggerhead turtle*. Finally, in the 1680s, it described a long-handled iron instrument with a bulbous end, used for heating liquids. It's the last sense that is thought to be the source for the modern expression, as it arose at the same time and it's possible that the implement was also used as a weapon.

long in the tooth
rather old

This phrase was first used to describe horses and comes from the way you can estimate a horse's age by looking at its teeth: if the gums have receded and the teeth consequently look very long, you know it's rather old. The same idea is found in the old proverb *don't look a gift horse in the mouth* meaning 'don't find fault with something you've been given'. Of course, it's not just in horses that gums recede with age: the process begins in middle age with humans too!

long time no see
it's a long time since we last met

The background to this familiar phrase would nowadays probably be regarded as rather questionable. It was originally an American expression and arose in the early 20th century as a supposedly humorous imitation of the broken English spoken by a Native American. Its dubious past has doubtless long been forgotten (if indeed it was ever widely known) and it is now freely used on both sides of the Atlantic.

a *loose* cannon

an unpredictable person or thing likely to cause unintentional damage

This expression sounds as though it could be centuries old, perhaps deriving from the days of Napoleonic warships. In fact, the first recorded uses are from the early 20th century and the phrase didn't really gain any true currency until the 1970s. That said, it does originate from the idea that a cannon which has broken loose from its mounting would be a particularly dangerous hazard on any ship, but especially a wooden one. In 2004 the BBC reporter John Pienaar observed of the Labour MP Clare Short, who had recently made controversial allegations about British spying activities, 'She is a loose cannon with a sense of direction.'

mad as a hatter

completely mad

Unfortunately, this expression has a sound scientific basis: in the past some hatters, or hat-makers, really did become mentally ill. Felt hats were made from fur, and one of the processes involved in their manufacture involved brushing a solution of mercurous nitrate on to the fur in order to make the fibres mat together. As a result of inhaling the mercury fumes, some hat-makers suffered from mercury poisoning, a nasty condition which can produce symptoms such as confused speech, hallucination, and loss of memory. The phrase 'mad as a hatter' was around in the 1830s, but it was of course popularized by one of the characters in Lewis Carroll's *Alice's Adventures in Wonderland* (1865), the Mad Hatter. Another phrase with the same meaning, *mad as a March hare*, arose from the excitable behaviour of hares at the beginning of the

breeding season. It was also reinforced by a character in *Alice's Adventures in Wonderland*: 'In that direction . . . lives a Hatter: and in that direction... lives a March Hare . . . they're both mad.'

far from the **madding** *crowd*

private or secluded

Most people associate this expression with the title of one of Thomas Hardy's classic novels, reinforced no doubt by John Schlesinger's film adaptation of 1967 starring Julie Christie and Alan Bates. In fact, Hardy took the title from a line in Thomas Gray's poem 'Elegy Written in a Country Church-Yard' (1751): 'Far from the madding crowd's ignoble strife'. Gray in turn may have been inspired by an even earlier poet, William Drummond, who in his sonnet 'Dear Wood' (1614) wrote: 'Far from the madding Worldling's hoarse discords'. Well, they do say that imitation is the sincerest form of flattery!

that way **madness** *lies*

that course of action will cause trouble

This is actually a quotation from Shakespeare's play *King Lear*, taken from a speech in which Lear shies away from contemplating the ingratitude of his daughters Regan and Goneril. The expression has become firmly established in general use, and doubtless not many people realize that they're reciting Shakespeare when they use it. In 2004 a BBC spokesman was quoted by the Reuters news agency as saying that the purpose of the BBC's complaints procedure was 'not to determine the truth—that way madness lies'.

a **man** *of the cloth*

a clergyman

The cloth was first used to refer to the clergy by the writer Jonathan Swift in 1710. A clergyman's 'cloth' had meant his profession since the mid 17th century, and before that other occupations which stipulated a special dress code or uniform had also been referred to as a person's 'cloth', notably that of lawyers and military men. These occupations still require a particular form of clothing to be worn, but only clergymen retain the description *men of the cloth*. The female equivalent *women of the cloth* is only slowly gaining currency, but give it time: old habits die hard!

tell that to the marines

used to express scornful disbelief

The *marines* were originally any men serving on board a ship, but later the meaning was restricted to troops who were trained to serve on land or sea, now particularly the Royal Marines or, in the United States, the Marine Corps. These facts, however, don't shed a great deal of light on the likely source of this expression. One suggestion is that it may have its origins in a remark made by Charles II: he advised that implausible tales should be checked out with sailors, who, being familiar with distant lands, might be the people best qualified to judge whether they were true or not. Another idea picks up the clue left in the longer version *tell that to the horse marines*. The horse marines were an imaginary troop of cavalry soldiers serving on board a ship, used as an image of total ineptitude or of people completely out of their natural element: the idea is that such people are so clueless that they'll believe anything they're told. The phrase is recorded from the early 19th century, but in 1823 the poet Byron noted that *that will do for the marines, but the sailors won't believe it* was 'an old saying'.

the real McCoy

the real thing

The source of this expression is far from clear: the trouble is that *McCoy* is a rather common surname and so there are numerous candidates for the post of the original McCoy. The earliest example of the phrase, dating from 1856, is Scottish, uses the form *Mackay*, and describes a brand of whisky: 'a drappie [drop] o' the real McKay'. The distillers G. Mackay and Co. apparently adopted *the Real Mackay* as an advertising slogan in 1870, and this was the form familiar to Robert Louis Stevenson, who used it to mean 'the genuine article' in a letter in 1883: 'For society, there isnae sae muckle [much]; but there's myself—the auld Johnstone, ye ken—he's the real Mackay.'

By the early 20th century recorded examples have the *McCoy* spelling and are American. Some of the uses still refer to whisky or other alcoholic drink, though the expression is described as coming from Canada: this is perhaps not so strange, as many Scots emigrated there. Other examples illustrate the more general current sense of 'the real thing'. One candidate for the title 'the Real McCoy' is Elijah McCoy, inventor of a machine for lubricating train engines and a lawn sprinkler. Possibly the favourite, however, is one Norman Selby, aka Charles 'Kid' McCoy. He was an American boxer who became welterweight champion in 1896 after knocking out Tommy Ryan, his sparring partner, to whom he had previously pretended to be ill and unfit. Apparently he often used this trick of feigning illness, only to appear fighting fit on the day itself, prompting commentators to wonder whether this was *the real McCoy*.

be mentioned in dispatches
be commended for your actions

The first uses of this phrase in its literal military meaning date back to the First World War, though of course the practice continues today. In official reports from the front line, any soldiers who have performed acts of particular bravery are commended by name. The phrase was later extended to anyone singled out for praise after some notable achievement or performance.

be on your mettle
be ready or forced to do your best in a demanding situation

The background to this expression is the highly variable state of English spelling up to the 18th century. Up to then the word *metal* was spelled in a variety of different ways, *mettle* being one of them. It had a range of meanings, from the solid material to 'personal quality', 'temperament', and 'courage'. Over time the spelling *mettle* came to be particularly associated with abstract meanings, and eventually people ceased to be aware of any connection between the two forms. The distinctive spellings were more or less fixed by the early 18th century, although some people persisted in spelling *metal* as *mettle* into the 19th century (but perhaps they were just bad at spelling!).

slip someone a Mickey Finn
give someone a drugged or doctored drink

Mickey Finn first came into use in the 1920s in America but soon became familiar across the ocean too, through the popularity of Hollywood films. It's generally thought that the original *Mickey Finn* was a notorious Chicago bartender who allegedly drugged and robbed his customers on a regular basis. One small doubt remains with this theory, however, and that is the fact that the first *Mickey Finns* weren't sedatives given to knock someone out, but something with a very different effect altogether: laxatives! So the alternative proposal is that bartenders in the rowdy Irish bars of 1920s America (where *Mickey Finn* would probably be a fairly common name) would get rid of troublesome drunks by slipping a laxative powder into their drink: a quick and easy way of getting your customers to leave at speed . . .

the **Midas** touch
the ability to make money out of anything you do

Midas was a king of Phrygia, an ancient region in Asia Minor, who ruled the country at the height of its power in the 8th century BC. According to Greek legend, Midas captured Silenus, the companion of the god Dionysus, but treated him well; because he had treated his captive so kindly, Dionysus granted him one wish. Midas asked to have the power of turning everything he touched into gold. At first this seemed a marvellous gift to have, but of course Midas very soon realized that he would starve to death, as even his food and drink turned to gold. He prayed to have the gift taken away and Dionysus, taking pity on him, told him that if he bathed in the River Pactolus (in modern Turkey) the power would be washed away. It's thought that the story may have originated to account for the presence of gold in the river.

a **millstone** around your neck
a heavy burden of responsibility

A *millstone* is a large circular stone traditionally used to grind corn, but the origins of this particular phrase lie in a far more unpleasant practice. The expression is thought to come from an ancient method of execution which involved throwing a person into deep water with a heavy stone attached to their neck. Several early Christian martyrs are believed to have suffered

this fate, and the method is also mentioned in the Bible in Matthew 18:6: 'But whoso shall offend one of these little ones which believe in me, it were better for him that a millstone were hanged about his neck, and that he were drowned in the depth of the sea.'

mind your Ps and Qs

be careful to behave well and avoid giving offence

People have been warned to *mind their Ps and Qs* since the 1770s, but the exact origins of the phrase are uncertain. One obvious suggestion is that it comes from a child's early days of learning to read and write, when they might find it difficult to distinguish between the two tailed letters *p* and *q*. Another idea suggests that printers had to be very careful to avoid confusing the two letters when setting metal type.

the **moment** *of truth*

a time when a person or thing is tested or a crisis has to be faced

This expression is a translation of the Spanish *hora de la verdad*, a term used in bullfighting. The first recorded use in English was by the writer Ernest Hemingway in his 1932 book *Death in the Afternoon*: 'The whole end of the bullfight was the final sword thrust, the actual encounter between the man and the animal, what the Spanish call the moment of truth.' The reason it is called the *moment of truth* is presumably that it determines which one of the combatants will die, although the odds would always seem to be against the bull in this situation.

a **month** *of Sundays*

a very long period of time

The source of this phrase is probably the apparently interminable nature of Sundays in the past, when various activities and certainly all forms of entertainment were strictly prohibited on religious grounds. Nowadays, of course, for many people Sundays are more or less indistinguishable from any other day of the week, marked out only by how quickly they rush past to arrive at Monday morning and the start of another working week.

the full monty

the full amount expected, desired, or possible

This expression became widespread following the success of the 1997 film *The Full Monty*, about a group of Sheffield steelworkers who become male strippers after being made redundant. The film highlighted a specific sense of the phrase, 'a full strip or total nudity', as in this example from an edition of the *Sunday Mirror* of the same year: 'Disappointingly, Steve doesn't get his kit off in *Ivanhoe*. "I'm bare-chested a couple of times, but not the full Monty," he says.' This particular meaning of the phrase is rather strange, given one of the suggestions for its origins. The theory in question proposes that it comes from *the full Montague Burton*, which was apparently a complete three-piece suit, named after a tailor producing made-to-measure clothing in the early 20th century: *the full monty* in this case was the complete opposite of total nudity! Another suggested source is the full English breakfast that Field Marshall Montgomery (nicknamed 'Monty') used to insist on each morning.

The trouble with these stories is that the expression is only recorded since the 1980s, and indeed none of the other suggested theories as to its origin are supported by reliable evidence. As with many phrases, we'll probably never know the truth.

over the moon

extremely happy

This expression, though it goes back to the early 18th century, is now particularly associated with post-match remarks from victorious footballers and football managers (along with its opposite, *sick as a parrot*). The origins of *over the moon* lie in another pastime popular with children, singing nursery rhymes. An old favourite contains the lines 'Hey diddle diddle, The cat and the fiddle, The cow jumped over the moon'.

a motley crew

a miscellaneous group of very different people or things

The word *motley* originally described a fabric woven from different-coloured threads and was later extended to refer to the multicoloured costume traditionally worn by a court jester in the Middle Ages. By the early 17th century the image of starkly contrasting colours and distinctive appearance had been developed to apply to any group consisting of a rather incongruous assortment of people or things, as in this extract from a synopsis of the film *The Full Monty*: 'Gaz . . . assembles a motley crew of his balding, overweight, and rhythmically challenged pals to take it all off to raise some fast money.'

break the mould

change to a markedly different way of doing things

The origins of this expression can be traced back to the manufacture of objects cast in moulds: destroying a mould afterwards ensured that no further copies could be made. The phrase dates back to the 1560s and probably comes from a translation of the Italian epic poem *Orlando Furioso*, written by Ludovico Ariosto in 1532: 'Nature made him and then broke the mould.' In 1980, one of the founders of the Social Democratic Party, Roy Jenkins, promoted the newly formed party as breaking the 'out-of-date mould' of British politics.

if the mountain won't come to Muhammad, Muhammad must go to the mountain

if one party refuses to compromise, the other party will have to make the extra effort

The story behind this proverb was told by the philosopher Francis Bacon in his *Essays* (1625). Muhammad was once challenged to prove his credentials as a prophet by summoning Mount Safa to come to him. Of course, the mountain didn't move an inch in response to his summons, but Muhammad had a ready answer for this. He observed that if the mountain had moved it clearly would have crushed him and all his followers to death; therefore it was only right that now he should go to the mountain and give thanks to God for his mercy in sparing them all from this disaster.

mum's the word

say nothing

This informal expression, and its familiar alternative *keep mum*, are perhaps most associated with the period around the Second World War, conjuring up spies and subterfuge and dark warnings about careless talk costing lives. In fact both phrases are much older, being recorded as far back as the early 16th century. The word *mum* itself was used on its own in medieval times to mean 'hush!' or 'shh!' As might be deduced from this last fact, *mum* originated as a representation of the sound you make when you close your lips firmly together and try to speak: it basically indicated either unwillingness or inability to say anything about a matter.

Murphy's law

if anything can go wrong it will

There have been various suggestions as to who the first *Murphy* might have been, but the most plausible traces the expression back to the US Air Force in the 1940s. In 1949 a certain Captain Edward Murphy was studying various aspects of deceleration at the Wright Field Aircraft Laboratory in Ohio. Clearly all did not go quite as smoothly as he had hoped, since in the course of his studies he apparently commented to a colleague that if things could be done wrongly, they would be. An edition of *Aviation Mechanics Bulletin* in 1955 went on to explain the theory as 'if an aircraft part can be installed incorrectly, someone will install it that way'. In 1962 the American astronaut John Glenn recalled a series of cartoons issued by the US Navy which featured a clumsy mechanic called *Murphy* 'who was prone to make such mistakes as installing a propeller backwards'. It seems rather unfortunate that Captain Murphy, who merely observed the phenomenon, should have had his name given to the hapless person responsible for the mistakes.

on the nail

(of payment) without delay

There have been various explanations over the years as to the source of this expression. It dates back to the 1590s, though there's an earlier Anglo-French equivalent which was in use in the 14th century. A popular suggestion as to its origins links it to the city of Bristol. Outside what used to be the Corn Exchange there are four large brass nails: apparently merchants would strike one of them to signal that a deal had been agreed and then pay up. Unfortunately, this explanation is unlikely to be true because the phrase was in existence before the nails in question. An alternative idea is that it comes from a now disused expression *to the nail*, which meant 'to perfection' or 'to the utmost'. It referred to the way that sculptors would make finishing touches to their work with a fingernail, or to joiners testing the accuracy of a joint in a similar way. The expression was perhaps used of paying up immediately to indicate that a transaction had been completed satisfactorily.

no names, no pack drill

punishment can't be given out if names and details aren't mentioned

Pack drill is a form of military punishment which involves making an offender perform parade-ground exercises while carrying a heavy backpack. This expression, dating back to the 1920s, was of course first used in army circles but soon came into more general use, especially as a joking aside advising someone to be careful how much they say about a particular person or matter.

not on your nelly

certainly not

This expression is first recorded in the 1940s as the longer version *not on your Nelly Duff*, which gives a small clue as to how it arose. It was originally rhyming slang, following a rather tortuous route which takes in *duff*, rhyming with *puff*, which in turn stands for 'breath of life', so ending up as an alternative version of *not on your life*. Phew! The existence of an actual person called *Nelly Duff* is debatable. *Nelly* was a common enough name, so it's perfectly possible. But then again, *duff* may simply have been taken from the informal word meaning 'of poor quality', and was perhaps just chosen at random to make a rhyme.

never-never land

an imaginary perfect place or situation

This expression is now usually associated with the imaginary country in J. M. Barrie's *Peter Pan* (1904), where Peter Pan and the Lost Boys live. Although the published text of the play actually calls the place *Never Land*, Barrie does refer to it elsewhere as *Never Never Land*. Barrie didn't in fact invent the phrase, as it has been used since the 1830s to refer to the remote and unpopulated northern part of the Northern Territory and Queensland in Australia: the original idea was that the area is so remote that a person might never return from it. More recently, *Neverland* was the name chosen by the pop star Michael Jackson for his mansion and estate in California, which even has its own amusement park.

his nibs

a mock title used to refer to a self-important man

The origin of this rather odd expression is uncertain. It is first recorded in the 1820s, although the version *his nabs* is found slightly earlier. The most likely explanation of its origins is that it comes from the slang word *nob*, meaning 'a wealthy or upper-class person', which sometimes took the form *nib*, as in the following quotation from P. G. Wodehouse's novel *Laughing Gas* (1936): 'You don't run to an English butler in Hollywood unless you are a pretty prominent nib.' The rhyming sound of 'his' with 'nibs' may be the reason that form was favoured in this particular phrase.

night of the long knives

a treacherous betrayal or ruthless action

The original *night of the long knives* happened many centuries ago in 472, when the legendary massacre of the Britons by the Saxons took place. According to the 12th-century Welsh chronicler Geoffrey of Monmouth, the Saxons attended a meeting armed with long knives, and when a prearranged signal was given each Saxon drew his weapon and slew the Briton seated next to him. The phrase is now more commonly associated with the murder of the leaders of the Nazi Brownshirts, carried out by the SS on Hitler's orders in June 1934. In Britain it is sometimes used of the occasion in 1962 on which Prime Minister Harold Macmillan dismissed a third of his Cabinet at the same time.

no-man's-land

an intermediate or ambiguous area of thought or activity

Back in the Middle Ages, *no-man's-land* was a piece of land that was neither owned nor inhabited by anyone. This meaning persisted over the centuries, but after the First World War the phrase became particularly associated with the ground between the German trenches and those of the Allied forces. The metaphorical use first arose in the mid 19th century with the sense of 'an imaginary place', and then developed the current idea of an area of ambiguity, as in: 'The farmers are caught in a no-man's land, between the free market and old-style Marxism.'

no news is good news

without information to the contrary, you can assume that nothing terrible has happened

This proverb sounds very modern, but actually it can be traced back at least as far as the time of King James I, who wrote in a letter in 1616 that 'No newis is bettir then evill newis'. A document of the same period suggests that it may be based on an Italian phrase *nulla nuova, buona nuova*, which literally translates as 'no news, good news'.

a nod's as good as a wink

there's no need for further elaboration or explanation

The longer version of this phrase, *a nod's as good as a wink to a blind horse*, is rather puzzling as the unfortunate horse would be unable to understand whatever signal the nodder or winker was attempting to convey. The use of *a nod and a wink* to mean 'a hint or suggestion' is recorded in 1710, several decades earlier than the proverb itself, which first appears in a letter written in 1793. It seems that the 'blind horse' was tacked on to the original phrase as a rather surreally humorous addition.

nosy parker

an overly inquisitive person

You might think twice about calling someone a *nosy parker* when you discover what its origins are! The first *nosy parker* is to be found in a postcard caption from 1907, 'The Adventures of Nosey Parker', which referred to a peeping Tom in London's Hyde Park. *Parker* is an old word for a park keeper, which dates back to the 14th century.

not in my backyard

not in the area close to where you live

This expression was first used in 1980 in the US as a rather derogatory way of describing the attitude of anti-nuclear campaigners, and quickly gave rise to the acronym *nimby*. In Britain it is associated by many people with the late Nicholas Ridley, the then Secretary of State for the Environment who in 1988 attacked country dwellers as selfish for opposing new housing developments, calling their attitude 'pure Nimbyism'. As it turned out, he himself was opposing the building of some new houses near his own country home.

nudge nudge
*used to draw attention to a
sexual innuendo*

Although catchphrases are often associated with comedy shows, few of these phrases make it into mainstream use. This expression, and the longer version *nudge nudge wink wink*, falls into this rare category, and we have Graham Chapman and friends of the 1970s British television show *Monty Python's Flying Circus* to thank for it. The show was first broadcast in October 1969 and the last episode appeared in December 1974, but in those five years the absurd and surreal style of humour had a great impact. The first printed use of the phrase appeared in the humorous magazine *Punch* in February 1973, and it continues to be popular with journalists and authors. This extract is from David Lodge's novel *Paradise News* (1991): 'This is the famous Waikiki beach. Haven't seen much of it yet—been catching up on our sleep (nudge, nudge).'

someone's number is up
*the time has come when
someone is doomed to die or
suffer disaster*

The first recorded use of this expression is by the English essayist Charles Lamb in a letter written in 1806, in which the context makes it very clear that the reference is to someone drawing a winning lottery ticket. Given that death or disaster don't seem particularly desirable prizes, other rather darker suggestions have been made as to the phrase's origins. One explanation links it to various passages in the Bible that refer to the 'number of your days', meaning the length of your life, and to expressions such as 'your days are numbered'. Another proposes that the number in question is a soldier's army number, associated with identifying casualties on the battlefield and the fatalistic expectation of a bullet with 'your name and number' on it.

in a nutshell
in the fewest possible words

A *nutshell* has been used since the late 16th century to symbolize compactness or brevity, although the current sense of this expression is only recorded from the 1820s. The idea is thought to have arisen from the supposed existence of a copy of Homer's epic poem *The Iliad* which was small enough to fit into an actual nutshell, mentioned by the Roman statesman and scholar Pliny (23–79 AD) in his work *Natural History*.

NAUTICAL EXPRESSIONS

As Britain is an island, with a long history of exploration and trading by sea and a famous navy, it's not surprising that many English phrases have a nautical origin.

Stormy seas

Although the British are notorious for talking about the weather, this isn't the only reason it's the source of several familiar phrases, as in the days before engine power sailing ships were very much at the mercy of the wind and storms. In seafaring circles, a ship would be described as 'making good or bad weather of it', referring to how well or badly it could cope with a storm. This gave rise to the more general expression **make heavy weather** of a task, meaning that you find it more difficult or complicated than it should be. Heavy weather literally means 'a strong wind together with driving rain and rough sea'. Bad weather at sea also gave rise to the phrase **be taken aback**. If a person is taken aback they're shocked or surprised; a ship, however, is taken aback when a sudden wind blows directly against its sails from the front and forces them against the masts. This prevents the ship from moving forward and also puts the masts at risk of being snapped in two.

Hoist the mainsail!

The different parts of a sailing ship also feature in several phrases. **Go by the board**, meaning 'be abandoned or rejected', originally described masts and bits of rigging that fell overboard, with the 'board' being the side of the ship. Someone **on their beam ends** is in a desperate situation, without any money or other necessities. The beams in question are the horizontal lengths of timber or metal which support the deck and join the sides of the ship together, so a ship on its beam ends has heeled over on to its sides and is in danger of capsizing. **Three sheets to the wind** is an informal term for 'drunk' ('two sheets' being a less well-known option, referring to someone who is only slightly tipsy!). In nautical use, 'sheets' are ropes attached to the lower corners of a sail, used to secure it or alter its direction. If they are 'to the wind' they are loose, and so the ship is impossible to control (as is a person who is drunk!).

Life on the ocean wave

Several phrases give us a clue as to what daily life at sea was like in times gone by. Someone who **swings the lead** is being lazy or shirking their duties. Swinging the lead actually involved lowering a piece of lead suspended on a string to find out the depth of the water. This was quite an important job but one which sailors perhaps sometimes did as slowly as possible to avoid being assigned a more strenuous duty! Sailors found guilty of more serious offences than laziness were liable to be flogged. This was likely to have been carried out using a type of whip with nine knotted cords, called a cat-o-nine-tails, or a cat for short. Conditions on board ship were of course very cramped, doubtless making it rather difficult to use this sort of whip with the desired force. These circumstances gave rise to the phrase **no room to swing a cat**, used to describe a very small or confined space. Another expression which may have arisen from the lack of space on board ship is **son of a gun**, an affectionate way of referring to a male friend, now used chiefly in North American English. The term was apparently first applied to boy babies born at sea to women who had been allowed to accompany their sailor husbands on a long voyage. The explanation behind it is that the baby had been born between the cannons on the gun deck, where the ordinary sailors often slept.

it makes no odds
it doesn't matter

At first glance you might suppose that this expression comes from the gambling sense of *odds*, as in 'odds of 8:1', but in fact its origins lie in an old use of the word, namely 'difference in advantage or effect'. A similar phrase is *what's the odds* meaning 'what does it matter', which is used especially in Irish English.

in the offing
likely to happen or appear soon

Offing is actually a nautical term for the more distant part of the sea visible from a harbour or anchoring ground. The wider use goes back to the late 18th century, with the first recorded example found in a letter written by the famous English potter Josiah Wedgwood in 1779. A more recent example comes from the American songwriter Ira Gershwin. Commenting on his reasons for dropping out of the City College of New York, he observed: 'In my second year I was still taking first-year mathematics and when I heard that calculus was in the offing, I decided to call it an education.'

hold out an olive branch
make an offer of reconciliation

A branch of an olive tree has long been an emblem of peace and goodwill, featuring in both classical mythology and biblical tradition. According to Greek legend, the goddess Athena presented the city of Athens with an olive branch to symbolize fertility and peace. In ancient Greece olive crowns were presented to winners in the Olympic Games and to worthy civic dignitaries, and brides would wear olive garlands. Probably the most familiar occurrence of the olive branch is in the story of Noah and the Ark in the Bible. A dove returns to Noah with an olive branch (or, more likely, given the size of a dove, an olive twig) to indicate that God is no longer angry and that the waters of the flood have begun to recede.

know your **onions**
be very knowledgeable about something

None of the explanations for the origin of this expression seem particularly convincing. The facts of the case are that the phrase was first used in the US, with the earliest written example occurring in a 1922 edition of *Harper's Magazine*. A number of similar phrases involving knowing a lot about foodstuffs were current at this time, and perhaps onions were the most popular or maybe the easiest to grow. Another idea is that *onions* is short for 'onion rings', which is rhyming slang for 'things'. This seems implausible, given the American origin, and the same goes for another theory doing the rounds, the C. T. Onions link. Dr Charles T. Onions worked on the first edition of the *Oxford English Dictionary* from 1895 and also went on to produce the *Oxford Dictionary of English Etymology* (1966). But however eminent a scholar he was, it's rather unlikely that his name would be widely known on both sides of the Atlantic.

open sesame
a free or unrestricted means of gaining or achieving something

The source of this expression is the story of Ali Baba and the Forty Thieves, popularly thought to be one of the tales of the *Arabian Nights* but actually first added to the text in a French translation from the early 18th century. In fairness to the French writer Galland, it is thought that he based his account on a tale handed down through traditional oral Arabic storytelling. In the story, Ali Baba discovers that *open sesame* are the magic words used to open the door of the cave where the forty thieves kept their treasure.

opportunity knocks
a chance of success occurs

The opportunity for success is presented in opposite ways in various related sayings. One positive view is that every person has a chance to succeed; the cautionary approach warns that *opportunity never knocks twice at any man's door.* Reflecting rather cynically many people's experience of life, the American cartoonist Doug Larson observed: 'Sometimes opportunity knocks, but most of the time it sneaks up and then quietly steals away.'

over-egg the pudding

go too far in embellishing or doing something

There are two problems associated with adding too many eggs when making a pudding (well, possibly three if you want to consider long-term health concerns). Firstly, it might not set or cook properly, so your marvellous dinner party will end on a rather disappointing note. Secondly, your pudding might emerge looking perfect, but it will be so rich that your dinner guests will feel hideously queasy after just a few mouthfuls. Either way, the old adage 'less is more' is one to remember, not just in the kitchen, but in other areas of life. In 1999 the *Financial Times* passed the following judgement on a swiftly repeated TV programme: 'Palin is certainly an engaging presenter, but the same show two nights in a row is over-egging the pudding.'

no pain, no gain

nothing is achieved without effort

English has long favoured the neat pattern of 'no this, no that' . The first recorded example, 'no penny, no pardon', found in a work by John Tyndale written in 1531, was a criticism of the Roman Catholic Church for its selling of papal indulgences. The phrase *no pain, no gain* became widespread following its use as a slogan in exercise classes in the 1980s, although the proverbial association of *pain* and *gain* has been around since the late 16th century. A recent example of the 'suffering to be beautiful' adage can be found in a headline in the *Washington Post* from August 2004: 'No Pain, No Gain. Can Shoe Designers Take the Hurt Out of Height?'

paint the Forth Bridge

used to indicate that a task can never be completed

The Forth Railway Bridge spanning the Firth of Forth in Scotland was built during the 1880s. Not only was it one of the first cantilever bridges ever constructed, it was also, for a time, the longest bridge in the world. Its steel structure, with its gigantic girders, has required continuous repainting ever since: it is so long and extensive that by the time the painters reach one end the other end is in need of another coat.

beyond the pale

outside the bounds of acceptable behaviour

A *pale* is a pointed wooden post used with others to make a fence, a sense which was soon extended to describe a fenced enclosure. In the past the *Pale* was a name given to various territories under

English control, especially the part of Ireland under English jurisdiction before the 16th century. The earliest reference to the Pale in Ireland, from the modestly titled *Introduction to Knowledge* (1547), stated that Ireland was divided into two parts, one being the English Pale and the other being 'the wyld Irysh'. It is widely believed that the Irish Pale was the source of *beyond the pale*, but this is actually not very likely, as the phrase is not recorded until the 18th century: its specific origin remains something of a mystery . A modern example of its use can be found in *Debrett's New Guide to Etiquette and Modern Manners* (1996): 'Traditionally it is beyond the pale to light up before the Loyal Toast.'

Pandora's box

a process that once begun generates many complicated problems

According to Greek mythology, Pandora was the first mortal woman. In one version of the story, she was created and sent to earth by the gods in revenge for Prometheus having brought back the gift of fire to the world. The gods had given her a box containing all human ills, which she foolishly opened, allowing them all to fly out. An alternative account has the box containing all the blessings of the gods, which would have been preserved for the world had she not allowed them to escape: the only blessing that remained was hope. The Labour statesman and trade unionist Ernest Bevin once issued a memorable warning about the Council of Europe: 'If you open that Pandora's Box, you never know what Trojan 'orses will jump out.'

paper *over the*
cracks
disguise a problem rather than
try to resolve it

Rather than a firm of painters and decorators, we have the German statesman Otto von Bismarck (or his translator, at least) to thank for this expression. Bismarck used the German equivalent of the phrase in a letter written in 1865, referring to a convention held at Gastein in Austria between Austria and Prussia. Tension had been rising between the two countries since their combined victory over Denmark in the previous year had given control of the duchy of Schleswig to Austria and that of Holstein to Prussia, but neither was quite ready to go to war. The Gastein deal gave a semblance of order to the situation, while in fact giving time for both to make preparations for an inevitable conflict.

be part *and*
parcel of
be an essential element of

Both parts (so to speak) of this expression have essentially the same meaning, as one of the earliest senses of *parcel* was 'a part'. The phrase was first used in the mid 16th century in legal documents (even then lawyers seem to have favoured using several words where one would do), but by the mid 19th century had crept into general use. The original sense of *parcel* is still retained in the use of the word as a verb meaning 'divide something into portions and share them out'.

go **pear-shaped**
go wrong

This informal expression was originally RAF slang, and though the first written examples are from the early 1980s, around the time of the Falklands War, it was probably in use several decades earlier. Its precise origins aren't entirely clear, but some sources suggest that it may have arisen as a darkly humorous reference to the shape of a fighter plane after it has nose-dived and crashed into the ground. A more cheerful alternative theory is that it describes a novice pilot's less than successful attempts to produce a perfect circle when performing acrobatic manoeuvres. The aircraft images are probably less well known than the popular assumption that the phrase comes from the idea of a woman putting on weight around her hips. A recent example reflecting this belief comes in an article from the BBC website discussing men's weight problems as they get older: 'Men's future goes pear-shaped'.

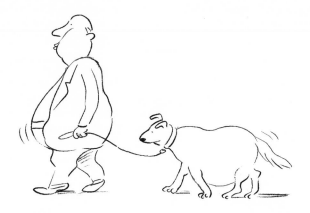

**keep your
pecker up**
remain cheerful

Although the origins of this British expression are quite innocuous, it has very different connotations in the US. The phrase has been around since the 1850s, and is even used by Charles Dickens in a letter written in 1857. It most probably comes from the comparison of a bird's beak to someone's nose, the idea being to encourage someone to keep their chin up and stop looking miserable. It's best to avoid using this phrase to urge an American acquaintance to cheer up, however, as *pecker* is a slang word for a man's penis in the United States!

**the penny has
dropped**
*someone has finally realized or
understood something*

This phrase is largely confined to British English but its origins lie in the gambling arcades seen the world over. The idea behind it is of a coin-operated slot machine whirring into action once a small coin has been inserted, with this being likened to someone's brain finally starting to work and make sense of something. The *penny* gives a clue as to the age of the expression, as it goes back to the 1950s. You'd probably have to say 'the pound has dropped' if you were coining the phrase nowadays!

go phut

fail to work properly or at all

At first glance, you might think that *phut* is just another word imitating a dull, abrupt sound, like *thud* or *clunk*, conjuring up the last gasps of a machine about to break down. In fact, the phrase was first used by Rudyard Kipling in *The Story of the Gadsbys* (1888): 'The whole thing went *phut*. She wrote to say that there had been a mistake.' Kipling was born in India, worked there as a journalist between 1882 and 1889, and set many of his writings in the India of the Raj. All this and the context in which he uses the phrase make it very likely that *phut* was actually an Anglo-Indian word from the Hindi and Urdu verb *phaṭnā* meaning 'burst'.

pie in the sky

something pleasant to contemplate but very unlikely to be realized

This expression was originally American and comes from a song written in 1911 by Joe Hill (1879–1915), one of the leaders of an organization called the *Industrial Workers of the World* (also known as the Wobblies). Along with their union card, each member would receive a songbook containing parodies of various popular songs and hymns of the day, with the motto 'To Fan the Flames of Discontent' on the cover. The song from which this phrase comes is called *The Preacher and the Slave*. It parodies a Salvation Army hymn called 'In the Sweet Bye and Bye' which promised those suffering on earth a better life in heaven. In response to the slave asking the preacher for some food, the chorus of the parody goes: 'Work and pray, live on hay, You'll get pie in the sky when you die.'

be someone's pigeon

be someone's concern or affair

This expression has nothing to do with homing pigeons going astray, or indeed anything involving that familiar bird. The phrase originally appeared with the spelling *pidgin*, which gives a better idea of its roots. A *pidgin* is a simplified form of a language such as English with some elements taken from local languages, and is used to enable people who don't share a common tongue to communicate with each other. The word originally represented a Chinese pronunciation of the English word 'business', and with the meanings 'business, occupation, or affair' became part of the simple language used between European and Chinese traders from the 1820s. By the 1850s *pidgin* was also being used to describe the language itself, especially in the fuller form *pidgin English*.

from pillar to post

from one place to another in an unceremonious or fruitless way

People were shunted *from post to pillar* back in the early 15th century, but for some reason by the middle of the following century the version *from pillar to post* came into use and soon became the favoured choice. Its origins lie in the ancient sport of real tennis. Real tennis is played in an enclosed court (a bit like the one used for squash, only much larger) with sectioned walls and buttresses off which the ball can rebound: hence the 'posts' and 'pillars' of the expression. It developed from an earlier game played by 11th-century monks in the cloisters of monasteries—conjuring up an image far removed from the usual one of hushed devout brethren!

in the pink

in very good health and spirits

Though you might well have rosy cheeks if you're *in the pink*, the expression has nothing to do with the colour of your complexion or with roses—though it is connected with another flower. A *pink* is a plant (called a 'dianthus' by botanists) with very sweet-smelling flowers which are usually various shades of pink, purple, or white: the use of *pink* for the colour beloved by little girls actually comes from the flower, rather than the other way round. Shakespeare uses the plant to signify the supreme example of something in *Romeo and Juliet*: 'I am the very pink of courtesy.' Here he was probably making a pun on the expression *the flower of something* meaning 'the finest part or individual'. This Shakespearean phrase led to the development of the phrase *in the pink of condition*, which in time was shortened to simply *in the pink*.

give someone the pip

irritate or depress someone

Pip is an unpleasant disease of chickens and other birds which is documented as far back as medieval times. From the late 15th century various human diseases and ailments also came to be called the *pip*, though the precise symptoms are rarely specified: today's equivalent would probably be the *dreaded lurgy* (a term possibly invented and certainly popularized by the 1950s radio comedy *The Goon Show*). Whatever the nature of the disease, the sufferer would probably be in a foul mood, hence the development of the sense 'ill humour'.

squeeze someone until the pips squeak

extract the maximum amount of money from someone

This expression was first used in a speech made in 1918 by the British politician Sir Eric Geddes on the subject of the reparations to be paid by Germany after the First World War: 'The Germans . . . are going to pay every penny; they are going to be squeezed as a lemon is squeezed—until the pips squeak.' Extracting money has always been popular with Chancellors of the Exchequer, and the Labour Shadow Chancellor Denis Healey was no exception when in 1974 he promised taxes that would 'squeeze the rich until the pips squeaked' if Labour were to win the forthcoming election, which they duly proceeded to do.

piping hot

very hot

Piping in this expression refers to the hissing and sizzling of very hot food just taken from the oven or off a fire. This phenomenon has been remarked on down the centuries, with the earliest recorded example being 'wafres pipyng hoot out of the gleede' ('wafers piping hot out of the fire') in Chaucer's *The Miller's Tale*.

be the pits

be extremely bad or the worst of its kind

Pits has been used since the 1960s as an informal shortened term for 'armpits'. These unfortunately often have a tendency to be damp and rather smelly and so it was but a small linguistic leap to have them symbolize the worst example of something. That's the nasty (and most likely) explanation. A more refined interpretation connects the bottom of a deep, dark hole with the lowest possible rank or class. Probably the most famous use of the phrase was by the tennis player John McEnroe in the 1981 Wimbledon championships: after various disputed calls and reprimands, he berated the umpire Ted James and other officials, yelling: 'You are the pits of the world!'

a *pitched* battle

a violent confrontation involving large numbers of people

Literally, a *pitched battle* is a battle fought between large formations of troops which is more or less confined to one location, as contrasted with a chance skirmish or a running battle. Originally, the time and place of battles were prearranged, which makes the business of conducting a military campaign seem rather like sorting out next season's football fixtures. As it turns out, the expression does nowadays tend to be used of football hooligans or violent protesters clashing with the police.

plain as a pikestaff

very obvious

The earlier version of this expression, dating from the 1540s, was *as plain as a packstaff*, which gives a small clue as to its origins. A *packstaff* was a long stick on which a pedlar used to carry his pack of goods for sale: the phrase may have arisen from the fact that this would be very obvious from a distance as the pedlar trudged along the road. By the end of the 16th century the current version with *pikestaff* was starting to be used and had more or less taken over a hundred years later. A *pikestaff* was a walking stick with a pointed metal tip: not clearly synonymous with being obvious, it has to be said. Possibly *pack* was simply adapted to *pike* because they sounded similar and pedlars were becoming a less familiar sight.

the *plot* thickens

the situation is becoming more complicated and puzzling

We can thank George Villiers, the 2nd Duke of Buckingham, for this particular expression. It's taken from his satirical drama *The Rehearsal* (1671): 'Now the plot thickens very much upon us.' The play mocks the heroic style associated with his contemporary John Dryden, who got his own back when he portrayed Villiers as the character Zimri in his satirical poem *Absalom and Achitophel* (1681).

point-blank

*(of a statement or question)
direct and without
explanation or qualification*

In literal use, *point-blank* is of course applied to a shot fired from very close to its target. The word *blank* formerly meant 'the white spot in the centre of a target', but this doesn't completely explain why *point-blank* should mean 'close to the target'. For this you need to know something about the trajectory of a shot fired from a gun: after a certain distance the bullet will follow a downward curve, so if you aim or *point* the gun directly at the centre of the target, you need to be sufficiently close for the shot still to be travelling horizontally as it hits the spot. The expression developed its general meaning back in the 1650s, only half a century after the shooting use arose, and tends to be used when asking about or refusing to do something, as in: 'He refuses point-blank to be photographed or give interviews.'

in **pole** position

*in a leading or dominant
position*

The origins of this expression lie in the world of sport, but not the first sport that comes to mind. Today it is of course used in motor racing to describe the leading position on the front row of the starting grid, which will allow the driver to take the first bend on the inside (assuming he makes it that far without colliding or breaking down). The phrase is often shortened to simply *in pole*, and it was in this version that it first came into use, long before the advent of the motor car. In the 1850s horse-racing pundits used the expression to refer to the starting position nearest the inside boundary rails. A century later motor racing took it over, and the extended use developed very soon after.

go **postal**

go mad, especially from stress

This informal expression is mainly used in America and is a fairly recent addition to the English language, with examples first found in the 1990s. It arose as a result of several reported cases that involved employees of the US postal service running amok and gunning down their colleagues. The headline of a newspaper article about a trial of all-postal ballots in local elections used the expression in a clever pun to emphasize the success of the experiment: 'Electoral apathy refuted as voters go postal.'

PARTS OF THE BODY

Different parts of the body have been used over
the centuries in a variety of phrases, especially to
represent certain human emotions or qualities.

Scenting trouble

A common theme in phrases featuring the nose is a person's
attitude or demeanour, which is usually one of haughtiness or
superiority. If you do something **with your nose in the air** you're
acting in a very supercilious way, and may well **turn your nose up
at** something, showing your distaste or contempt for it. These
expressions may have arisen from the way someone recoils from a
repulsive smell—or a whiff of the great unwashed! The idea of
being above someone, or better than them, is also contained in
the expression **look down your nose at someone**, meaning 'despise
someone'. The way animals such as pigs use their snout to sniff
out and root about for food has prompted various
phrases to do with curiosity, or 'nosiness'. So,
for example, we have the warning to
keep your nose out, given to someone
with a tendency to **poke their nose
into** other people's business. The
image of an animal following a
scent is also behind the more
positive expressions **follow your
nose**, meaning 'trust your instincts', and **a nose for** something,
meaning 'an instinctive talent for something'.

The eyes have it

The eyes are often used to represent awareness or acceptance of
something. The expression **close** or **shut your eyes to something** is
used to describe the behaviour of someone who refuses to
acknowledge an unpleasant or unwelcome fact. On the other hand,
if you do something **with your eyes open** it means that you're fully

aware of the possible consequences of your actions. As well as having the power of sight, the eyes are very expressive of our emotions. When we're amazed by or very interested in something, our **eyes are out on stalks**. If you **make eyes at someone**, you look at them in a way that shows you find them sexually attractive.

Mouthing off

Another facial feature that indicates how we are feeling is of course the mouth. When we smile, turning up the corners of our mouth, it shows we are happy. If we do the opposite, it shows we are dejected or **down in the mouth**. Although the teeth are often displayed when smiling, they tend to represent fierceness or power in phrases. **Showing your teeth** means revealing your strength or the power you have over someone, and nowadays we frequently hear calls for organizations and regulatory bodies to be **given teeth**, meaning that they should have genuine power to impose punishments for offences committed. The expression **get your teeth into something**, meaning 'work energetically and productively on a task', paints a picture of a ferocious animal gnawing hungrily on a carcass.

A helping hand

We use our hands for many different types of work, and this has prompted several phrases. If we **give someone a hand**, we help them do something. Someone who is **a dab hand** is an expert in a particular activity. 'Dab' was once used on its own to mean the same thing, and although its origins aren't certain, it may be connected with the idea of dabbing on paint with skill and dexterity. The image of someone skilfully wielding a paintbrush leads us to another common theme to do with hands: control and its opposite, freedom. If you **have your hands tied** you're prevented by circumstances from acting in the way you wish. Conversely, if you're given **a free hand**, you have the freedom to act completely at your discretion. However, a situation which gets **out of hand** is one in which those in charge have lost control.

go to pot

deteriorate through neglect

This expression dates back to the 1530s, and early examples have the meaning 'be ruined or destroyed'. The image behind it wasn't one of cannibalistic practices or some inedible stew cooked up by an incompetent chef, but simply referred to ingredients being chopped up and put in a pot ready for cooking. The idea of something deteriorating through neglect probably arose from pots being used for slow, gentle simmering, as contrasted with something being fried in a pan or roasted on a spit, both of which required regular attention.

*your **pound** of flesh*

something you are owed, but which it is ruthless to demand

Shakespeare's play *The Merchant of Venice* is the source of this expression. In the play the moneylender Shylock lends Antonio, a merchant, a sum of money but demands in return a pound of Antonio's flesh if he fails to repay the debt on time. When the due date arrives Shylock insists on holding him to the agreement, and Antonio is only saved by the clever pleading of his friend's wife Portia. She argues that if the flesh is taken, it must be done without shedding blood, as this isn't mentioned in the deed. An article from *The Guardian* illustrates the sort of context in which the phrase is often used today: 'The new bankruptcy law, critics charge, will give banks the leverage to squeeze every last pound of flesh out of debt-stricken consumers even if it means they lose their homes and cars.'

pour oil on troubled waters

try to settle a dispute with placatory words

The belief that oil can calm rough seas goes back at least two thousand years: the Roman scholar Pliny (23–79 AD) mentions the use of oil by sailors in his encyclopedic work *Natural History*. The idea remained part of folklore until the American statesman and inventor Benjamin Franklin determined to establish the truth of the matter in a famous experiment carried out on the large pond at Clapham Common in London. In a letter of 7 November 1773 he described how 'the oil, though not more than a teaspoonful, produced an instant calm over a space several yards square'. Incidentally, by recording the way that the oil spread over a large but finite area, and then stopped spreading, Franklin unknowingly indicated a way of estimating the size of molecules.

a *pricking* in your thumbs
a premonition or foreboding

This expression comes from a speech by the Second Witch in Shakespeare's play *Macbeth*: 'By the pricking of my thumbs, Something wicked this way comes.' Thumbs have long been associated with the supernatural in various ways: for example, holding your thumb by folding it into the palm of your hand is an old method of warding off evil or (to put a positive spin on it) bringing good luck. The practice is mentioned by the Roman poet Ovid (43 BC–*c*17 AD) and is still in evidence today.

pull the plug
prevent something from happening or continuing

Probably the first image that comes to mind with this expression is of someone disconnecting an electrical device by pulling out the plug from the socket. In fact, the phrase pre-dates by twenty years the first electric lamp, developed almost simultaneously in 1879 by Joseph Swan in England and Thomas Edison in America. The plug referred to in the phrase is actually one used in an old-fashioned type of toilet: in the days before modern cisterns the toilet had to be flushed by pulling up a stopper (or plug) to empty the contents of the pan into the soil pipe. Interestingly, the first recorded example of the literal meaning of *pulling the plug* was by Florence Nightingale in *Notes on Nursing* (1859): 'As well might you have a sewer under the room, or think that in a water closet the plug need be pulled up but once a day'. (Not a pleasant image.) The wider meaning developed in the 1930s, and with advances in toilet technology and the extension of electrical power to the home, the connection to the original use was soon forgotten. The following example comes from the magazine *EuroBusiness*: 'Faced with potential losses of around £35 million, the banks backing the project decided to pull the plug.'

pull strings

use your influence and contacts to gain an advantage

An American version of this expression is *pull wires*, and the image behind both forms is that of a puppeteer controlling the movements of a marionette by means of its strings. Sometimes this idea is brought to the fore, as in this headline from *The Observer* of 27 October 2002: 'Who was pulling the strings of [the] Chechen terrorist leader?'

pure as the driven snow

completely pure

Driven snow is snow that has been formed into drifts by the action of the wind. The colour white has long been a symbol of purity and the perfectly smooth, unblemished appearance of snowdrifts reinforces the association. The American actress Tallulah Bankhead (1903–68), whose colourful and uninhibited personality was legendary, famously parodied the phrase in 1947: 'I'm as pure as the driven slush.'

born to the purple

born into a reigning family or privileged class

Purple was originally a crimson dye extracted from a particular shellfish. It was very rare and expensive and so only royal and imperial families could afford to wear garments of this colour. The actual colour of the dye could vary widely and so over time the word came to be used for a colour between red and blue. The alternative expression *born in the purple* may have originated from the room in the imperial palace at Constantinople (modern Istanbul) in which empresses traditionally gave birth: the walls of the room were lined with the purple stone porphyry.

a Pyrrhic victory

a victory won at too great a cost

The word *Pyrrhic* comes from *Pyrrhus*, the name of a king who from around 307 to 272 BC ruled over Epirus, an ancient country forming part of present-day Greece. Pyrrhus invaded Italy in 280 and managed to defeat the Romans at the battle of Asculum in 279, though only after sustaining very heavy losses. After the battle he is said to have exclaimed: 'One more such victory and we are lost.'

cut someone to the quick
upset someone very much

The *quick* is the soft, tender flesh below the growing part of a fingernail, toenail, or, in animals, a hoof. Farriers might talk of trimming down a horse's hoof *to the quick* and some people of a particularly nervous disposition bite their nails right down *to the quick*. This area of flesh is well supplied with nerves and so is very painful when injured, and a transfer from physical to mental pain is a natural development. The very specific application of *quick* to this part of the body developed from an earlier meaning: 'living' or 'alive' (as in *the quick and the dead*), as contrasted with dead or inanimate.

call it quits
agree that terms are now equal or that enough has been done

Nowadays, *call it quits* is a fairly informal expression, especially when used to mean 'decide to abandon an activity', but its early history lies very much in officialdom. Church records of accounts from the late 15th century use the word *quits* to indicate that money owing to someone has been paid in full, and this gives a clue as to its origins. In medieval times church business was usually conducted in Latin, and so *quits* probably arose from a scribe's shortening of the medieval Latin word *quittus*, meaning 'discharged', which was written on receipts to indicate that the goods had been paid for. The current expression dates back only to the 1890s but an earlier version, *cry quits*, is recorded from the 1630s. Today the phrase is often used of people abandoning a job, or of couples ending a relationship, as in 'After a called-off wedding, Ben Affleck and Jennifer Lopez finally called it quits in January.'

on the qui vive
on the alert or lookout

This expression is of course French in origin and literally means 'live who?', that is, 'long live who?' In the past a sentry would issue this challenge to someone approaching his post to find out where their allegiance lay. Depending on the answer given, the person would either be allowed in or dragged off to a dungeon. As a security measure, it seems a little flawed: you'd have to be a very incompetent spy not to know the preferred response.

rack *your brains*

make a great effort to think of or remember something

The origins of this expression are decidedly grisly. A *rack* was a medieval instrument of torture consisting of a frame and rollers to which the victim's wrists and ankles were tied. As the rollers were turned, the prisoner would be gradually stretched until their arms and legs were dislocated. To *rack* someone was to torture them on this device: the gruesome image behind the phrase is that of subjecting your brain to a similar ordeal in trying desperately to remember something.

ragtag *and bobtail*

a disreputable or disorganized group of people

Almost every possible permutation of the main elements of this expression has been used over the centuries. It originally involved three words and occurred in the versions *tag, rag, and bobtail* (Samuel Pepys's *Diary*, 1659), *rag, tag, and bobtail* (Byron's 'The Blues', 1820), and *tagrag and bobtail* (Dickens's *Barnaby Rudge*, 1840), before the current one with *ragtag* finally emerged as favourite. *Bobtail* didn't vary as it was an established term for a horse or dog with a docked tail, but *rag* and *tag* were separate words conveying the same meaning of 'tattered or ragged clothes'. Putting them together (in whatever way you fancy) gives you the literal sense of 'people in ragged clothes together with their dogs and horses'.

rain *cats and dogs*

rain very hard

This expression is first recorded in Jonathan Swift's *Polite Conversation* (1738), a humorous compendium of proverbs, sayings, and clichés, but an alternative version *rain dogs and polecats* is found around a century earlier in Richard Brome's *The City Witt* (1653). The fact that the earlier version doesn't feature cats is rather awkward, as most of the speculative explanations of the phrase's origins focus on our feline friend. Cats have long been associated with witches, typically having the role of familiar and credited with the ability to cause storms. A witch was also said to assume the form of a cat when riding on a storm. Dogs too have a place in mythology, with Odin, the Norse storm god, depicted with dogs as attendants and the wind having the head of a dog in old German legends. Despite all this, neither cats nor dogs (nor polecats, for that matter) seem particularly keen on wet weather, and it may be that the true source of the phrase is much more mundane. It's possible that in the past a few gullible people might have believed that drowned cats and dogs floating in flooded streets had fallen from the skies during a previous heavy downpour. Possible, but not probable, it must be said.

take a **rain** check

refuse an offer, reserving the right to take it up at a later date

The origins of this phrase, which is mainly used in North America, lie in a system that could usefully be adopted elsewhere. Literally, a *rain check* is a ticket issued to spectators when a sporting fixture or other outdoor event is interrupted or postponed by rain. The ticket allows admission on another occasion or enables the holder to claim a refund of their entrance money. The system was operating at least as far back as the 1880s, but the extended meaning didn't develop until the 1930s.

a **rainy** day

a possible time in the future when money will be needed

This expression, which dates back to the 1580s, may originate from the need of casual farm labourers to be especially careful with their money and set aside a certain amount literally for *a rainy day*. If the weather was bad, they were unable to work—and if they didn't work, they didn't earn any money.

take the **rap**

be punished or blamed, especially for something that's not your fault

Rap was originally a slang term in use among American criminals, with various meanings from 'a criminal charge' to 'a prison sentence', and featured in a number of expressions such as *beat the rap*, meaning 'escape a prison sentence' and *take the rap*, meaning 'accept the responsibility and punishment for a crime'. It's likely that it came from a use of *rap* to mean 'a criticism or rebuke', which in turn probably developed from the idea of someone receiving the punishment of a sharp blow with a stick for a minor misdemeanour. The expression *a rap across the knuckles* is often used today to mean 'a mild reprimand'.

blow a raspberry

make a rude sound with the tongue and lips, to express scorn or contempt

This apparently inoffensive expression actually originated as *blow a raspberry tart*, which is of course rhyming slang for 'a fart'. Both *raspberry* and *raspberry tart* date back to the 1890s, quite a bit earlier than the American equivalent *a Bronx cheer*: this wonderfully sarcastic term (originating from the tough New York City borough *the Bronx*) didn't surface until the 1920s.

read the riot act

give someone a severe warning or reprimand

The *Riot Act* was passed by the British government in 1715 in the wake of the Jacobite rebellion of that year and was designed to prevent civil disorder. The Act made it an offence for a group of twelve or more people to refuse to disperse within an hour of being ordered to do so and after having been read a certain section of the Act by a person in authority. This last requirement created something of a problem, as actually reading it aloud wasn't the easiest thing to do in the middle of a genuine riot, and many of the arrested often claimed that they hadn't heard it being read. (It's doubtful whether this ever proved a successful defence, however.) The Act failed to prevent a number of major disturbances in subsequent years, but despite this it wasn't repealed until 1967.

ours not to reason why

it's not your place to question a situation

This expression comes from a line in Tennyson's poem 'The Charge of the Light Brigade' (1854): 'Their's not to make reply, Their's not to reason why, Their's but to do and die'. The poem describes a notorious incident in 1854 during the Battle of Balaclava in the Crimean War. A misunderstanding between the commander of the Light Brigade, Lord Cardigan, and his superiors, Lord Raglan and Lord Lucan, led to the British cavalry mounting a suicidal attack down a valley held on three sides by the Russian forces. The charge resulted in the loss of almost half of the Light Brigade to little or no military effect.

a **red** herring

something, especially a clue, that is misleading or distracting

Herrings have been caught and eaten in various guises for centuries, but one of the fish's drawbacks is that it starts to go off very quickly and so needs to be preserved to keep it edible. Today, the most familiar version of a preserved herring is a kipper, which is cured by smoking and turns brown in the process. To extend herrings' shelf life even further, though, you can combine two curing methods: if they are steeped in salt water and then smoked, they turn a dark red colour and keep for months. But how do we get from salty red fish to misleading clues? Well, in addition to being red, herrings treated in this way are also very hard and very smelly, and an alternative role seems to have been found for them. Back in 1686, a book entitled *The Gentleman's Recreation* describes foxhounds being trained to follow a scent by huntsmen dragging a red herring over the ground. This practice may have been modified to dragging the herring across a fox's trail to test whether the hounds would be distracted by an alternative scent. From this it is but a small step to the meaning familiar today, though a slight problem is that the earliest example of the phrase doesn't appear until 1884: the whole story could just be a complete *red herring*!

put on the **ritz**

make a show of luxury or extravagance

This phrase invokes the name of hotels in Paris, London, and New York founded by the Swiss-born hotelier César Ritz (1850–1918). These grand hotels became synonymous with great luxury, especially during their heyday in the 1920s. The first recorded example of the expression dates back to 1926, but it gained widespread popularity following its use in the Irving Berlin song 'Puttin' on the Ritz' (1929), which featured in a film of the same

name in 1930. The best-known version of the song is a performance by Fred Astaire in the 1946 musical *Blue Skies*.

sell someone down the river

betray someone, especially so as to benefit yourself

The origins of this expression lie in the Deep South of the United States. It originally referred to the practice of selling troublesome slaves to the owners of sugar-cane plantations on the lower Mississippi, where conditions were harsher than those in the more northerly slave-owning states. The first recorded use is in 1851 by the American writer Harriet Beecher Stowe, whose best-known work is the anti-slavery novel *Uncle Tom's Cabin* (1852). The book's descriptions of the sufferings caused by slavery greatly strengthened the abolitionist movement. The 'betray' sense didn't emerge until much later, in the 1920s, perhaps because the subject was too sensitive to make light of.

rob Peter to pay Paul

take something away from one person to pay another

This is a very old expression, going as far back as the late 14th century, but its precise origins aren't clear. It probably refers to the saints and apostles Peter and Paul, who are often shown together as equals in Christian art and so might be regarded as being equally deserving of religious devotion. The alliteration of their names, both beginning with 'P', may also have swung the balance in their favour. Although the earliest examples feature robbery, other versions have cropped up over the centuries, such as *unclothe Peter to clothe Paul* and *borrow from Peter to pay Paul*. This last alternative probably helped in the development of the phrase's additional meaning 'pay off one debt only to incur another'.

smoke-filled rooms

used to refer to political decision-making conducted privately by a small group of influential people

The source of this expression is a 1920 news report on the Republican nominations for the US presidency: 'Harding of Ohio was chosen by a group of men in a smoke-filled room.' The nominee, Warren G. Harding, was something of a dark horse and a lack of openness and democracy was associated with his selection. *The Economist* recently used the expression in a report in 2004 on a forthcoming lawsuit against the top cigarette manufacturers: 'That is what the tobacco men were up to, says the government, when they met on December 15th, 1953 in a doubtless smoke-filled room in a New York hotel, and schemed to mislead the public about the risks of smoking.'

room at the top

the opportunity to join the top ranks of a profession

This expression is attributed to the American politician and lawyer Daniel Webster (1782–1852), who was advised against trying to enter the overcrowded legal profession and is said to have replied: 'There is always room at the top.' The phrase was taken up in the early 20th century and was used as the title of John Braine's first novel, published in 1957, about an ambitious young man in an industrial town in the north of England.

show someone the ropes

teach someone the established way of doing something

The origins of this expression go back to the mid 19th century and the days of sailing ships. Skill in handling ropes and tying knots was of course essential for any sailor, and the idea was soon extended to other walks of life. A range of variations on the theme developed, including *learn the ropes* and the more familiar *know the ropes*.

a rough diamond

a person of good character who lacks manners or education

Literally speaking, *a rough diamond* is a diamond before it has been cut and polished. The metaphorical use reflects the idea that beneath an unprepossessing exterior lies something of great value. The first example is to be found in 1700 in John Dryden's preface to his collection of fables, in which he remarks: 'Chaucer, I confess, is a rough diamond', possibly an observation on the down-to-earth (if not downright rude) language to be found in the *Canterbury Tales*. The American equivalent of the phrase is *a diamond in the rough*.

rub someone's nose in it

emphatically draw someone's attention to an embarrassing fact

This expression goes back to the 1920s, although the alternative version *rub it in* crops up a little earlier, in the 1870s. The obvious question is, what is the 'it' that your nose is being rubbed in? Something not very pleasant at all, is the answer. The expression comes from a misguided way of house-training puppies or kittens: literally rubbing their noses in any malodorous deposit they may make in the house in an attempt to dissuade them from repeating the offence.

rule the roost

be in complete control

At first glance, this expression would seem to refer to the pecking order that exists among chickens, with the chief fowl bossing around the others in the roost. There may be some truth in this explanation, but it's not the whole story, because the phrase originated as *rule the roast* in the 15th century, some 300 years earlier than the modern version. The most plausible explanation for its origins is that the phrase referred to the most important person at a banquet or feast. How *roast* changed to *roost* remains a mystery.

run high

(of feelings) be intense

Feelings have been *running high* since the early 18th century, just as long as rivers and seas have been described as running high too. The literal use describes a river flowing strongly and about to burst its banks or a stormy sea well above the usual height. Both are images that evoke the idea of emotions out of control or about to spill over into confrontation or violence, as in this example from a report on Afghanistan by CNN Online: 'Tensions are running high with any sounds, particularly in the night, raising fears that an attack may have begun.'

run of the mill

ordinary or undistinguished

A *run* is the quantity of something produced at one time, and the *run of the mill* is the material produced from a mill before it has been sorted or inspected for quality. The mill referred to is in fact a cotton mill, as opposed to one that grinds corn for flour: goods such as sheets used to be sold as *run of the mill*, indicating that they could not be guaranteed to be flawless and so were effectively being 'sold as seen'. Both the literal and metaphorical uses arose in the early 20th century, with an alternative version *run of the mine* also featuring, especially in early examples.

a **running** battle
a dispute that has gone on for a long time

Literally, a *running battle* is a battle that is constantly changing its location, as opposed to a pitched battle that takes place in one (originally prearranged) place. The expression first occurred in the late 17th century as *running fight* and described a naval engagement in which the fighting continued even as one side was fleeing. The current version *running battle* is not recorded until the 1960s but is now the more common, even in non-military contexts, as in: 'A hard-working widowed father of three . . . has had a running battle with the immigration authorities for 15 years.'

in a **rut**
following a fixed pattern of behaviour that is hard to change

A *rut* is a long, deep groove made by the wheels of vehicles repeatedly travelling along the same track. It can be very difficult for a vehicle (unless it's a four-wheel drive, of course!) to follow any course other than the one already worn down, and this is the image behind the phrase, which made its first appearance back in the 1830s, courtesy of the historian and political philosopher Thomas Carlyle (1795–1881). A similar expression emerging around the same time is *in a groove* but it didn't catch on to the same extent.

your **salad** days

the time when you were young and inexperienced

This expression is one of Shakespeare's inventions, occurring in *Anthony and Cleopatra*. The idea behind the phrase becomes clearer when you read the full line spoken by Cleopatra: 'My salad days, When I was green in judgement'. Shakespeare used the word *salad* in a clever pun on the word *green*, which is still used today in the sense 'inexperienced or naive'.

sit below the **salt**

be of lower social standing

This expression goes back to the days when formal dinners were more commonly held and when a person's rank determined where they sat at the table. Long dining tables running the length of the room were the norm and those of the highest rank sat at the top end of the table, with the others arranged in descending order of status along the remaining length. The salt cellar was usually placed halfway down, and so anyone sitting below it knew they had a long way to climb before they made it to the A-list!

behind the **scenes**

in private

The *scenes* in this expression are the pieces of scenery on a theatre stage. The area behind them is where the actors wait to go on stage and where the means of moving various props are located, all of which should remain hidden from the audience. The extended senses of privacy and secrecy developed in the 1740s, and the expression is now widely used to talk of activities out of the public eye, as in this recent example from the *Belfast Telegraph*: 'Contacts have been continuing behind the scenes since the meeting between Mr Ahern and Mr Blair in London last week.'

from **scratch**

from the very beginning, without making use of any previous work

The origins of this expression lie in the sporting world. In the past certain sports such as cycling and running sometimes used a particular handicap system. A line or mark, known as the *scratch*, was drawn to indicate the starting position for all competitors except those who had been awarded an advantage: they were allowed to start a little way in front. So, a competitor starting *from scratch* would start from a position without any advantage. The expression *up to scratch*, meaning 'up to the required standard', also comes from this practice, as originally it referred to someone who was good enough to start from the scratch line.

by the **seat** of your pants

by instinct rather than logic or knowledge

American pilots in the 1940s were the first to use this expression. They used to talk about *flying by the seat of their pants*, meaning that they flew the plane using their instinct and experience rather than relying on the aircraft's instrument panel. The idea was that an experienced pilot could tell by a change in the vibrations of the seat if, for example, the plane was about to stall, and so take early action to rescue the situation. The phrase was soon extended to all sorts of activities, as in this example: 'He takes so many cases that he's sometimes flying by the seat of his pants in court—relying on the quick study to cover up for lack of preparation.'

sell your soul

do anything, no matter how wrong, to achieve your objective

The longer version of this expression is *sell your soul to the devil* and it refers to tales of deals supposedly struck with the devil. Over the centuries various people reputedly agreed to give their soul to the devil if in return he would grant them all their heart's desires in this life. The most famous person alleged to have made such a pact was the 16th-century German astronomer and necromancer Faust. His story was published in 1587 and soon translated into English, where it inspired Christopher Marlowe's play *Doctor Faustus*. Two centuries later the great German writer Goethe made Faust the subject of a poetic drama, and fascination with Faust continued into the 20th century, his actions being linked to Nazism in a novel by Thomas Mann.

shades of —

used to suggest that one thing is reminiscent of another

The origins of this expression have nothing to do with colour, but in fact go back to an old use of *shade* meaning 'a ghost'. The idea behind the phrase is that the person or event either resembles or calls to mind someone or something from the past. By the late 19th century the meaning 'ghost' was more or less restricted to works of literature, so it's rather odd that it should have been revived in this phrase in the mid 20th century. Nonetheless, it's very familiar nowadays, as in this example from the American magazine *Town & Country*: 'Shades of Jackie O, the Duke and Duchess, Capote, and an era when classic French cuisine, spacious luxury, and swizzle sticks were de rigueur.'

on Shanks's pony

on foot

This expression is based on a pun with the surname Shanks and the now informal term *shanks* meaning 'legs', which originally came from an Old

continues on page 156

SHAKESPEARE'S PLAYS

As one of the world's greatest playwrights, it's no surprise that Shakespeare should have had a great influence on the English language. His legacy can be seen in the remarkable number of phrases attributable to him which are widely used today.

To be or not to be?

The famous 'to be or not to be' soliloquy in HAMLET is a very productive source of English phrases. In the speech Hamlet debates the great question of existence itself, and whether it is right to commit suicide. He talks, for example, of **the slings and arrows** of 'outrageous fortune', describing the adverse factors or circumstances that come our way in our daily lives. The 'sling' in this expression is a type of weapon consisting of a strap to hurl stones. The passage has also given us the expression **shuffle off this mortal coil**, meaning 'die', and the observation **there's the rub**, meaning 'that is the crucial difficulty'. Here, the word 'rub' is a term used in the game of bowls for any obstacle that alters the course of a bowl.

Hoist by your own petard

Shakespeare was writing over 400 years ago and many of the terms he used are unfamiliar to us today. Some of these are preserved in phrases we have borrowed from his plays, such as **at one fell swoop**, meaning 'all in one go'. It comes from Macduff's appalled reaction to the murder of his wife and children in MACBETH: 'Oh hell-kite! . . . . All my pretty chickens, and their dam At one fell swoop?' The image is clearly of a kite (a bird of prey) swooping down, but the word 'fell' is rather more obscure. It dates back to medieval times and means 'very evil', with the more familiar word 'felon' also having the same Old French source. Another peculiar phrase is **be hoist by** or **with your own petard**, which means that your plans to cause trouble for others end up backfiring on you. The phrase again originates in HAMLET and both its main elements are puzzling to a modern speaker. The word 'hoist' is in fact the past participle of the old dialect verb 'hoise' which meant 'lift or remove', while a petard was a small bomb in the form of a metal or wooden box filled with gunpowder. Someone who was literally 'hoist with their own petard' was blown into the air by their own bomb.

A word in your ear

Although we might not realize it, we have Shakespeare to thank for some very familiar English expressions. **Have a word in someone's ear** is a more interesting way of saying that you'll speak to someone discreetly, especially to give them a warning. It comes from MUCH ADO ABOUT NOTHING: 'Come you hither, sirrah; a word in your ear, sir'. Someone who is described as being **made of sterner stuff** is better able to overcome problems than others. The expression was first used in Mark Anthony's description of Julius Caesar: 'When that the poor have cried, Caesar hath wept; Ambition should be made of sterner stuff: Yet Brutus says he was ambitious; And Brutus is an honourable man.' Shakespeare seems to have been pleased with his invention **to your heart's content**, as it features in two of his plays, HENRY VI, PART 2 and THE MERCHANT OF VENICE, in the sense 'complete inward satisfaction'. Nowadays we use it to mean 'as much as you want to'. Someone who has treated another person harshly may justify their actions by saying they are being **cruel to be kind**. The first person to use this line of reasoning was Hamlet, explaining why he bullied his mother about her second marriage, a marriage that has taken place only a month after his father's death.

English word meaning 'shin bone'. It was first used by the Scottish poet Robert Fergusson in 1785 in the version *shanks-nag*; another alternative is *on Shanks's mare*, now common in North America. The phrase is typically used as a wry observation regarding a person's inability to afford any means of transport other than their own two feet.

lick someone OR something into shape
act forcefully to bring someone or something into a better state

The origins of this expression go back to early medieval times when books called bestiaries were popular. A bestiary was an early sort of reference book giving information and observations on different kinds of animal. Some of these bestiaries described how bear cubs were supposedly born as formless lumps and were literally licked into shape by their mother. This belief seems to have persisted for some time, as the current use doesn't appear until the early 17th century. Since then other versions including *knock* and *whip someone into shape* have come into use, possibly reflecting the former popularity of corporal punishment as a parenting tool.

separate the sheep from the goats
divide people or things into superior and inferior groups

This expression is a biblical reference to the account of the Last Judgement in Matthew 25:32–3, which describes how all the nations of the world will be gathered before God and how 'He shall separate them one from another, as a shepherd divideth his sheep from the goats: And he shall set the sheep on his right hand, but the goats on his left.'

when someone's ship comes in
when someone's fortune is made

This expression goes back to the mid 19th century when Britain dominated the world of maritime trading. The safe arrival of a ship carrying a valuable cargo meant an instant fortune for the owner and any others with shares in the enterprise. Going overboard with nautical allusions, a report in *Scotland on Sunday* on the Olympic gold-medal-winning cyclist Chris Hoy was headlined 'Hoy attracts attention as his ship comes in.'

shipshape and Bristol fashion
in good order

Clearly this expression is nautical in origin, but the details of its development are less clear. The *shipshape* part is fairly straightforward, as it comes from the orderly layout of a ship's equipment and rigging: sailors would serve on many different ships, so it was essential that they knew immediately where to find the gear. *Bristol fashion* provides more of a subject for debate. It seems likely that it originated from Bristol's rather awkward location on the River Avon, some six miles from open water. Ships would come into the port on the tide and would soon become stranded as the tide receded, putting considerable strain on their structure. One suggestion is that Bristol shipbuilders knew they had to ensure that their ships were particularly sturdy and well maintained in order to withstand the testing conditions of the port, but of course any ship coming into Bristol would suffer in the same way. An alternative explanation connected with the cargo seems more likely. The Bristol dockers would be aware that they had to be careful to load and unload cargo in an orderly way, otherwise the uneven distribution of weight would put even further strain on the ship as it just sat on the mud, unsupported by water.

as sick as a parrot
extremely disappointed

A variety of animals have cropped up over the centuries in phrases emphasizing how ill someone is feeling. The first was the dog, back in the early 18th century. Dogs often seem to represent bad things: you can be *dog tired* and have *a dog's dinner* (which might well make you as *sick as a dog*). Other comparisons include the horse and the cat, the latter being well known for its problems with hairballs, of course. All these phrases refer to physical sickness, whereas being *sick as a parrot* is a mental thing, to do with feeling depressed about something. This version goes back to the 1970s, and is particularly associated with despondent footballers and football managers being interviewed after a crushing defeat (the opposite is of course *over the moon*). It's possible the phrase originated as a reference to the famous sketch about a dead parrot in the television series *Monty Python's Flying Circus*; it's almost always been used with tongue in cheek.

the sick man of —
a country that is poor or unsound in comparison with its neighbours

The first country to be described in this way was Turkey, back in the late 19th century. The expression arose following a reported comment by Tsar Nicholas I of Russia about the Sultan of Turkey in 1853: 'I am not so eager about what shall be done when the sick man dies, as I am to determine with England what shall not be done upon that event taking place.' His remarks reflected the precarious state of the Ottoman Empire and its slow but inevitable disintegration. The term was applied to other countries over the following decades, and now often refers to factors other than economics or politics. This example from *The Scotsman* exploits the literal meaning of the phrase: 'Scotland remains the "sick man of Europe" in terms of smoking-related diseases, with some 13,000 deaths and 33,500 hospital admissions each year.'

in your sights
within the scope of your ambitions or expectations

The sport of shooting has given us this expression, with the *sights* in question being a device on a gun which helps you aim at the target more precisely. The implication is that you are firmly focused on achieving your ambition: the same idea is found in *raise* (or *lower*) *your sights*, meaning 'become more (or less) ambitious' and *set your sights on something*, meaning 'have something as an ambition'.

the silver screen
the film industry

This expression goes back to the early days of film-making and is recorded from the 1920s. Literally, a *silver screen* was a projection screen covered with metallic paint to give it a highly reflective silver-coloured surface. Nowadays, *the silver screen* tends to be used to refer to the golden age of Hollywood films in the 1930s and 1940s.

at sixes and sevens

in a state of total confusion and disarray

The origins of this expression lie in gambling with dice. Betting on the fall of dice has been popular for centuries, and the phrase first occurs in Geoffrey Chaucer's poem *Troilus and Criseyde* (1385), in the version *set on six and seven*. It's most likely that the phrase was a fanciful alteration of the Old French words for five and six, *cinque* and *sice*, these being the highest numbers on a dice. The idea was that risking all your worldly goods on the possibility of these two numbers coming up was the height of recklessness, and could result in your whole world falling apart.

knock someone for six

utterly surprise or overcome someone

Those familiar with the game of cricket will know that a *six* is a hit that sends the ball clear over to the boundary without first striking the ground, scoring six runs. Obviously, the ball needs to be struck with a mighty whack to travel as far as that, and this is the image behind this expression. The idea is that a piece of news or some other event leaves you feeling as dazed as if you'd been given a hefty blow with a cricket bat. The phrase is also found in the form *hit someone for six*, which tends to have the slightly different meaning of 'affect someone very severely', as in 'The beef industry was hit for six by the BSE crisis.'

hit the skids

begin a rapid decline or deterioration

This expression and the similar *put the skids under someone or something*, meaning 'hasten their decline or failure', both originated in the US. The word *skid* is a North American term for a wooden roller that is used as part of a set to move logs or other heavy objects. Once a log is on the skids it can be slid forward very easily, gathering momentum until it reaches the end of the rollers and comes to an abrupt halt. *On the skids* is also used to describe someone whose career is in a bad state. The term *skid row*, meaning 'a run-down part of town frequented by tramps and alcoholics', is also connected with logging. It originated as *skid road* and at first simply described a part of town frequented by loggers, presumably notorious for being rough, tough, hard drinkers.

come up *smelling* of roses

emerge from a difficult situation with your reputation intact

The longer (and ruder) version of this expression is *fall in the shit and come up smelling of roses*. As all good gardeners know, rose bushes need plenty of manure to ensure that they flourish and flower prolifically. That said, however marvellous a show of flowers a freshly mulched rose bed might produce, you really would have to be very lucky to land in one and still smell remotely pleasant!

a *smoking* gun

a piece of indisputable evidence

The scenario of someone standing holding a smoking gun next to a corpse with gunshot wounds is a favourite one from detective novels and films. Sir Arthur Conan Doyle's Sherlock Holmes story 'The Gloria Scott' (1893), for example, features the line 'the chaplain stood with a smoking pistol in his hand'. Pedants might suggest that such a situation makes for a rather short whodunnit, but that aside, a recently fired gun (unlikely still to be smoking) is a useful piece of evidence and provides a vivid image. The phrase really came to the fore during the Watergate scandal in the early 1970s involving the US Republican president Richard Nixon, who was implicated in a break-in at the Democratic Party headquarters. When a tape revealed Nixon's wish to limit the FBI's role in the investigation into the incident, Republican congressman Barber T. Conable famously observed: 'I guess we have found the smoking pistol, haven't we?' More recently, the expression has been used in connection with the search for weapons of mass destruction in Iraq: the existence of these weapons was used to justify the US-led invasion in 2003, with Condoleezza Rice, then the US national security adviser, stating: 'We don't want the smoking gun to be a mushroom cloud.'

a *snake* in the grass

a treacherous or deceitful person

Snakes have been associated with treachery since the 6th century BC and the fables of the Greek storyteller Aesop. In one of Aesop's stories a farmer finds a snake stiff and frozen with cold. He puts it close to his chest to warm it up, but as soon as the snake revives it bites him. Early uses of the snake as a metaphor for treachery in English tend to hark back to Aesop and feature snakes and bosoms: examples with *grass*, implying an unseen or unknown source of danger, don't actually occur until the late 17th century. The equivalent phrase before that had featured toads, which in past times were thought to be poisonous: a treacherous person was called *a pad in the straw* (*pad* is an old dialect word for a toad). The current expression may have originated from a Latin poem by the Roman poet Virgil.

cock a snook
openly show contempt for someone or something

If you literally *cock a snook* you place your hand so that your thumb is touching your nose and your fingers are spread out: if you feel really contemptuous you can waggle you fingers (and possibly say 'yah boo sucks!' at the same time). The gesture is very ancient, occurring under a variety of names across the world, and is of course still very common today—though usually only among children! The actual expression is only recorded from the 1790s, and unfortunately there are few definite clues as to its origins. The meaning of *cock* is probably connected to the modern sense 'tilt something at an angle'. As for *snook*, it may be an alteration of *snoot*, an informal term for the nose (and the source of the adjective *snooty* meaning 'contemptuous'). In 2004 *Time Out* observed of the British fashion designer Vivienne Westwood: 'For all her cocking a snook at the establishment, Westwood's always wanted mainstream approval.'

for a song
very cheaply

This expression was first used in the early 17th century and probably comes from the old practice of selling copies of ballads very cheaply at fairs. The alternative version *for an old song* was also used, perhaps because the latest 'hits' of the day were more expensive, with only the golden oldies on special offer. The phrase gained new popularity when it was used in *Going for a Song*, the title of the recently revived 1970s television quiz show that requires teams to guess the date and value of various antiques.

SPORT

Sport plays a major part in many people's lives, and has done over the centuries, even if the sports we follow have changed. Many phrases that were once restricted to the speech of the true fan have in the course of time crept into more general use.

Some knockout examples

One of the older spectator sports is boxing, with its popularity well documented from the 1800s. The many rules and regulations involved in boxing are reflected in a couple of expressions in general use. The phrase **saved by the bell** is often used when someone has avoided an awkward or embarrassing moment by the lucky intervention of some event or remark. It comes from the situation in a boxing match where a contestant who has been knocked down can be saved from being counted out by the ringing of the bell marking the end of the round. A boxer who has been knocked unconscious might be described as **down and out**, but in general use the phrase has developed a very different sense, referring to someone who is without money, a job, or a place to live.

The sport of kings (and queens)

Horse racing has also produced its fair share of English phrases. In a very close race, the horses may be described as being **neck and neck**, meaning that they are exactly level. The expression is now also used in other types of racing and in other competitive situations such as political elections. If someone wins a contest **hands down** it means they had a very easy and decisive victory. This phrase comes from the posture of a jockey in the closing stages of a race. If he was so far ahead that he was certain of victory, instead of continuing to urge on his horse he could lower his hands and relax his hold on the reins. One phrase which at first glance seems to have no connection with horse racing is **warn**

someone off. In general use it means 'order someone to keep away from somewhere or stop doing something', but it is in fact a shortened version of 'warn someone off the course'. Up until 1969, the British Jockey Club had a rule that allowed it to prohibit someone who had broken its regulations from riding or running horses at meetings under the Club's jurisdiction.

On your marks . . .

Athletic events have generated their own group of phrases. In many running races the atheletes have to stand with their feet just behind a white line marked on the track. This was known as **toeing the line**. The sense was extended more generally, so that nowadays if you won't **toe the line** it means that you refuse to accept the authority or principles of a particular group, even under pressure. The white line also features in the expression **be quick (or slow) off the mark**, where the 'mark' is another word for the starting line. In everyday use this phrase describes someone who is fast (or slow) at responding to a situation, or who is quick (or slow) to understand what is meant. To signal the start of a race a starting pistol is fired and runners who set off before this are said to have made **a false start** or to have **jumped the gun**. Outside sports commentaries **a false start** is used to describe an unsuccessful attempt to begin a task or project, while someone who **jumps the gun** does something before the appropriate time.

sour grapes

an attitude of pretending to despise something because you can't have it yourself

The source of this phrase is the tale of the fox and the grapes, one of the famous fables of Aesop, a Greek storyteller of the 6th century BC. In the story a fox tries to reach a bunch of juicy grapes hanging from a vine high above his head. After several attempts he gives up and stalks off, saying 'I'm sure the grapes are sour anyway.'

spike someone's guns

thwart someone's plans

This expression first arose in the mid 17th century, a busy time for soldiers, what with the English Civil War (1642–9) and the Anglo-Dutch Wars (1652–72). The phrase described the practice of hammering a metal spike into any cannon captured from the enemy. The spike was driven into the small hole through which the charge was ignited, thereby rendering the gun useless as it couldn't be fired.

be the spit of

look exactly like

There are a number of variations of this phrase, which dates back to the early 19th century, including *the very spit*, *the dead spit*, and *the spit and image*. *Spitting image* is based on the last version, and probably arose because *spit* itself was no longer widely understood. The basis of the association between *spit* and resemblance is not wholly clear. Various early examples of use (from the 1600s) describe one person as being so like another that they could have been spat out of their mouths—though why spitting should entail likeness remains unclear. One suggestion brings in ancient witchcraft, the idea being that witches could conjure up an exact likeness of someone using a drop of that person's saliva. It has to be said that this explanation is more imaginative than plausible!

spit *and* sawdust

(of a pub) old-fashioned or run-down

Up until the mid 20th century it was the norm for pubs to have a public and a saloon bar, the former being more basic and cheaper than the latter. The floor of the public bar would often be sprinkled with a layer of sawdust, which would soak up spillages in general and customers' spit in particular. The habit of spitting in public has become socially unacceptable and so, thankfully, referring to *a spit-and-sawdust pub* is now only exaggeration.

put a **spoke** *in* **someone's wheel**

prevent someone from carrying out a plan

At first glance this expression appears to make no sense at all: spokes are, after all, something of an essential component of most wheels. However, a closer look at the history of the phrase sheds some light. Early examples from the 1580s onwards featured spokes being put in objects other than wheels, for example cogs, the turning of which would definitely be hindered by an inserted spoke. These alternatives had disappeared by the 18th century, after which *wheel* prevailed. The explanation probably lies in a parallel Dutch phrase which used the word *spaak* meaning 'a bar or stave', together with the Dutch equivalent of 'wheel'. Given these facts, the most likely explanation is that the phrase was originally based on a mistranslation, which centuries of English speakers have cheerfully but illogically perpetuated.

win the wooden **spoon**

be last in a race or competition

Winners of the wooden spoon nowadays are usually teams in sports such as rugby and hockey, and they don't have their humiliation compounded by being awarded an actual spoon. Not so for the unfortunate candidate coming last in the final examination in mathematics at Cambridge University: back in the early 19th century he would actually be presented with a wooden spoon, to symbolize his 'wooden-headedness' or stupidity.

square the circle

do something that is considered to be impossible

The literal meaning of *square the circle* is 'construct a square equal in area to a given circle', a problem which is incapable of a purely geometrical solution. The puzzle has taxed the brains of mathematicians for thousands of years, with one of the earliest attempts to solve it mentioned in an ancient Egyptian papyrus. Greek mathematicians wrote at length on the subject, and the idea must have caught the public's imagination as it even features in one of Aristophanes plays, *Birds*, written in 414 BC. The earliest example in English comes from outside the world of geometry, in a 1624 sermon by the poet and preacher John Donne.

stake a claim

assert your right to something

This expression originated in America at the time of the California gold rush of 1849, when prospectors would register their claim to a particular plot of land by marking out the boundary with wooden stakes driven into the ground: this was called *staking a claim*. From the late 19th century the phrase came to be used in a wide variety of contexts, and now that there is little left without an owner, land is perhaps one of the least likely things that a person would be staking a claim to.

steal someone's thunder

win attention for yourself by pre-empting someone else's attempt to impress

The source of this expression is surprisingly literal. The English dramatist John Dennis (1657–1734) invented a method of simulating the sound of thunder as a theatrical sound effect and used it in his unsuccessful play *Appius and Virginia*. Shortly after his play came to the end of its short run he heard his new thunder effects used at a performance of Shakespeare's *Macbeth*, whereupon he exclaimed: 'Damn them! They will not let my play run, but they steal my thunder!'

let off **steam**

get rid of pent-up energy or strong emotion

The invention of the first practical steam engine by Thomas Newcomen in the early 18th century, later improved on by James Watt, didn't just have an impact on people's working lives and surroundings: it provided the English language with numerous new expressions. The literal meaning of *let off steam* is 'release excess steam from a steam engine through a valve', vital in preventing the engine from blowing up. The meaning which is familiar today arose in the 1830s in the alternative version *blow off steam*: the phrases reflect the idea that it's as important for people to give vent to feelings of tension or stress as it is for steam engines to release excess pressure. A related image is found in the phrase *have steam coming out of your ears*, meaning 'be very angry'.

stiff upper lip

a quality of uncomplaining stoicism

Although this expression describes a characteristic typically associated with the British, it apparently originated in North America. The earliest recorded example is from the American writer John Neal's novel *The Down Easters* (1833): 'What's the use o' boo-hooin'? . . . Keep a stiff upper lip; no bones broke.' The perception of stoicism as a peculiarly British quality is reflected in the use of the phrase in the title of one of P. G. Wodehouse's best-loved books about upper-class Bertie Wooster and his butler, *Stiff Upper Lip, Jeeves* (1963). Quite why the upper lip should remain rigidly unmoving is something of a mystery, as generally speaking it's the bottom lip that starts to wobble at times of crisis.

still small voice

the voice of your conscience

This expression comes from the Bible, dating back to the 1611 King James version. In 1 Kings 19:12 the prophet Elijah is hiding out in a cave, but is told to come out and hear the word of God. First of all a great wind comes, then an earthquake, and finally a fire: 'And after the earthquake a fire; but the Lord was not in the fire: and after the fire a still small voice.' Later versions of the Bible use the phrase *a sound of silence* instead.

in stitches
laughing uncontrollably

The word *stitch* goes back to Anglo-Saxon times, when it was used to describe any sharp stabbing pain; only later was it restricted to the current sense of 'a sudden sharp pain in the side caused by strenuous exercise'. Shakespeare seems to have been the first to mention a stitch brought on by laughing, when he used an alternative version of the expression in *Twelfth Night*: 'If you . . . will laugh yourselves into stitches, follow me.'

be set in stone
be fixed and unchangeable

This expression and the alternative versions *be carved* or *written in stone* all refer to the biblical story of Moses and the Ten Commandments. According to Genesis 31:18, God wrote the Commandments on tablets of stone and handed them down to Moses on Mount Sinai. The phrase tends to be used of rules or decisions that can't be changed. In 2004 *The County Wedding Magazine* cautioned brides-to-be: 'You can't get stuck into the arrangements until the date's set in stone.'

pull out all the stops
make a tremendous effort to achieve something

The *stops* in this expression are the knobs or levers on a church organ which control each of the different sets of pipes. If you pull out a stop it allows the air to flow through the pipes and produce the sound. *Pulling out all the stops* will obviously result in the full range of pitch and the maximum volume possible. The metaphorical use of the phrase first emerged in the 1860s, and the additional meaning 'do something very elaborately or on a grand scale' developed soon after. The following example is taken from a 1992 edition of the *Financial Times*: 'Party organizers pulled out all the stops in bringing supporters to the polls. "No-one who said they would vote for us didn't vote for us, unless they were dead," Mr Watts said.'

the **straight** and narrow

the honest and morally acceptable way of living

The earliest examples of this expression were in the longer version *the straight and narrow path* or *way*. The phrase actually arose through a misunderstanding of the meaning of a word in the Bible: Matthew 7:14 reads 'Strait is the gate, and narrow is the way, which leadeth unto life.' *Strait* is in fact just another way of saying 'narrow', an old sense which only really survives today in the noun meaning 'a narrow passage of water connecting two seas', as in *the Straits of Gibraltar*. The confusion probably came about because *crooked*, the opposite of *straight*, had long been used to mean 'dishonest'.

the last OR final straw

a final minor difficulty that makes a situation unbearable

This expression comes from the old proverb *it is the last straw that breaks the camel's back*. The first indication of its familiarity is in Charles Dickens's novel *Dombey and Son* (1848): 'As the last straw breaks the laden camel's back, this piece of underground information crushed the sinking spirits of Mr. Dombey.' Other variations on the theme were in use earlier, however, notably *the last feather breaks the horse's back*, which dates back to the mid 17th century.

have many **strings** to your bow

have a wide range of resources that you can make use of

The origins of this expression lie in the sport of archery, although of course archery was originally less a sport and more of a necessary skill in warfare and hunting. In either situation it was a good idea for an archer to have a spare string or two, just in case the one already strung in his bow should break. The use of the phrase outside the world of archery dates back to the 1520s, in the version *have two strings to your bow*: other alternatives have come into use over the centuries, for example *have* or *add another string to your bow* meaning 'have a further resource that you can make use of'. The veteran entertainer Nicholas Parsons had this piece of advice for budding actors when interviewed in 2004: 'Most people in our profession stick to one thing. If you do one thing, say get on to a TV soap or something, you may become famous quicker, but when that dries up what do you do then? You must have another string to your bow.'

the sun is over the yardarm
it's the time of day when it's socially acceptable to drink alcohol

This is an old nautical expression going back to the late 19th century. A *yardarm* is the end section of a *yard*, a thick tapering pole slung across a ship's mast for a sail to hang from. The time in question is noon, when the sun is at its highest point in the sky, not 6 o'clock as is often supposed (presumably by those disapproving of a lunchtime snifter or thinking of a *sundowner*, a drink taken at sunset). The earliest example of the phrase comes from a series of travel articles by Rudyard Kipling, published under the title *From Sea to Sea* (1899): 'The American does not drink at meals as a sensible man should . . . Also he has no decent notions about the sun being over the yard-arm or below the horizon.'

surf the net
move from site to site on the Internet

With the remarkable spread in the use of the Internet over the past decade, this expression has rapidly become a very familiar part of the English language, although the earliest recorded example is from as recently as 1992. It originates from the American expression *channel-surfing* (the British tend to *channel-hop*). This term describes the practice of constantly switching from channel to channel using a television remote control in the (often vain) hope of finding an interesting programme. *Channel-hopping* emerged first in the late 1970s, but American users seem to have decided a decade later that it was much cooler to be a *channel-surfer*, a term that evokes an image of freedom and ease of movement.

swear like a trooper
swear a great deal

A *trooper* was originally a private soldier in a cavalry unit. The term was first used in 1640 in connection with the Scottish Covenanting army, who were fighting against Charles I's attempt to impose the Anglican Church on them and quash their own form of religious organization, Presbyterianism. It was then used of troops in the English army in 1660. At some point these soldiers developed a terrible reputation for lewd behaviour and bad language, a view which was clearly widespread by the 18th century: in his novel *Pamela* (1739–40), Samuel Richardson writes 'She curses and storms at me like a Trooper.'

sweet *Fanny*
Adams
absolutely nothing at all

Fanny Adams was the young victim in a brutal murder of 1867, her body being mutilated and cut up by her killer. With gruesome black humour, by the end of the century her name had became a slang term in the Royal Navy for a type of tinned meat or stew that had recently been introduced. The current meaning arose in the early 20th century and is sometimes shortened to *sweet FA*. The *FA* here is widely thought to stand for the F-word and the word *all*, but in fact the expression is perfectly respectable.

sweet *spot*
a particularly fortunate
situation or factor

The *sweet spot* is an informal term used in various sports to describe the area on a bat, club, or racket at which it makes most effective contact with the ball. Its actual existence has been open to question, but recent research by a physicist at the University of Sydney in Australia suggests that the *sweet spot* has a scientific basis and is not a myth after all.

sword *of Damocles*
an imminent danger

Damocles was a courtier who, according to legend, told Dionysius I, ruler of Syracuse in Sicily (in the 4th century BC) that he must be the happiest of men, being so wealthy and powerful, and wished that he could be in his shoes for just one day. Dionysius granted his wish and invited him to a banquet where he was treated like a king. Halfway through the festivities, however, he happened to glance up and saw a sword suspended by a single hair right above his head: Dionysius had given him a graphic demonstration of how fragile his happiness was, living as he did under constant fear of assassination. In 1994, following various allegations concerning the probity of the administration of the US Democrat president Bill Clinton, the *American Spectator* magazine remarked: 'A dozen swords of Damocles dangle over the heads of Democrat candidates for the House and Senate—they dread opening next morning's paper.'

to a T OR **tee**

to perfection

This expression dates back to the late 17th century, but how it arose is not certain. Various ideas as to what the *T* stands for have been put forward, ranging from a golfer's tee to a builder's T-square, but none is totally convincing. Another possibility is that it originated from the action of completing a letter T with the horizontal stroke (as in the phrase *dot the i's and cross the t's,* meaning 'make sure all the details are correct'). The problem with these explanations is that the expression occurs earlier than the proposed sources. One suggestion that is historically possible, however, is that it is a shortened version of the early 17th-century phrase *to a tittle,* which has exactly the same meaning as to a *T*. A *tittle* was a small stroke in writing or printing, such as the crossbar of a 'T' or the dot of an 'i', which fits the idea perfectly.

turn the tables

turn a position of disadvantage into one of advantage

In the past the word *table* was applied to the board used for games such as chess, draughts, or backgammon, and *tables* came to refer specifically to backgammon because its board has two folding halves. Although this meaning had died out by the mid 18th century it is preserved in this expression, which arose from the common practice of turning the board round between games so that a player had to play from what had previously been their opponent's position. The idea of a reversal of positions is nicely illustrated in this example from *Glamour* magazine: 'Penélope turned the tables on the paparazzi and took their photograph from the red carpet.'

in **tandem**
alongside each other

In Latin *tandem* means 'after a long time' or 'at length'. In the late 18th century the word came to be used in English as a jokey slang term for a carriage drawn by two horses harnessed one behind the other (a much longer set-up than if they were harnessed side by side!). *Tandem* quickly became the standard way of describing the carriage and pair, the pair of horses themselves, and the way of driving (as in *drive tandem*). With the demise of the carriage, a *tandem* is now most familiar as a bicycle for two riders, one behind the other. The expression *in tandem* is still used today to mean 'one behind another', but is more common in the sense 'together as a team', as in this example from the *Daily Telegraph*: 'Giammetti has worked in tandem with the designer since Valentino launched his own house in Rome in 1960.'

a **tangled** web
a complex and difficult situation

This expression comes directly from Sir Walter Scott's epic poem *Marmion* (1808): 'Oh what a tangled web we weave When first we practise to deceive!' The 20th-century American humorist Ogden Nash was one of many to pick up the phrase in his observation on parenthood, 'Oh, what a tangled web do parents weave When they think that their children are naïve.'

have someone OR something **taped**
understand someone or something fully

The earliest examples of this expression appear in the early 20th century, unfortunately without any obvious clues as to its origins. It may come from the idea of a tailor measuring a customer with a tape measure and so knowing all about their height, girth, and so on. Alternatively, the image may be of tying someone up with tape and so having them under complete control. The only thing that's certain is that it has no connection with recording on tape, as that meaning doesn't appear until the 1950s.

bush *telegraph*

a rapid informal network by which information or gossip is spread

This expression originated in the Australian outback in the late 19th century. *Bushrangers* were outlaws who lived out in the bush, hiding from the authorities. They used to rely on a network of informers, nicknamed the *bush telegraph*, to warn them about the movements of the police in their vicinity. By the 1940s the expression had spread beyond Australia to apply to any informal network that passed on information.

on *tenterhooks*

in a state of suspense or agitation because of uncertainty about a future event

A *tenter* is a frame on which fabric can be held taut so that it doesn't shrink while drying or undergoing some other treatment during the manufacturing process. (Incidentally, it comes from the same Latin word meaning 'stretched' that *tent* comes from.) *Tenterhooks* were the hooks or bent nails used to fasten the fabric in position. This procedure had obvious appeal as an image for a person in difficulties or suspense, at first (from the mid 16th century) in *on (the) tenters* and later (from the mid 18th century) in *on tenterhooks*, which soon superseded the original form. The phrase has survived long after real tenterhooks disappeared.

throw in the towel

admit defeat

The origins of this expression lie in the boxing ring. Boxers or their trainers traditionally signal that they are conceding defeat by throwing the towel or sponge used to wipe the contestant's face into the middle of the ring. The earliest version of the phrase is *throw up the sponge*, dating from the 1860s; *throw in the towel* appears around half a century later.

thumbs up
an indication of satisfaction or approval

This expression and its opposite *thumbs down*, meaning 'an indication of rejection or failure', hark back to the days of Roman gladiatorial combat. The thumbs were used to signal approval or disapproval by the spectators, though they actually used *thumbs down* to indicate that a beaten gladiator had performed well and should be spared, and *thumbs up* to call for his death. The reversal of the phrases' meanings first appeared in the early 20th century.

on tick
on credit

The *tick* in this expression is a shortening of *ticket*, used in the old phrase *on the ticket*. The *ticket* in question is an IOU promising to pay the money due, but there is also the suggestion of a pun on the reputation of moneylenders as 'bloodsucking parasites'. Both *on tick* and *on the ticket* date back to the 17th century, when credit was obviously as popular as it is today.

as tight as a tick
very drunk

The bloodsucking parasite sort of *tick* is the source of this expression, although, as in the previous phrase, punning is also a feature in its development. The alternative version *as full as a tick* is first recorded in the 1670s and refers to the way ticks swell as they gorge themselves on blood. Both forms of the phrase have the additional meaning 'be full after eating', but the more recent *tight as a tick* plays on two senses of *tight*: it can mean both 'drunk' and 'stretched taut', as a tick is after it has had its fill of blood.

on the tiles
having a lively night out

This expression is first recorded in a dictionary of slang published in 1887, so was probably around a decade or so earlier. The image conjured up is of a cat out on the rooftops at night, caterwauling and generally having a good but noisy time: just like the average Friday night out on the town!

time and tide wait for no man

if you don't make use of a favourable opportunity, you may never get the same chance again

The word *tide* in this proverb has been interpreted since the 16th century as 'the tide of the sea': a sailing ship must leave with the outgoing tide or be delayed by at least six hours and possibly more. Originally, however, *tide* was just another word for *time* (surviving in terms like *Yuletide* and *Whitsuntide*), and the two were first used together just as repetition for effect.

time immemorial

a time in the past so long ago that people have no memory of it

Both this expression and its equivalent *time out of mind* were originally legal formulas. The exact meaning was 'a time beyond legal memory' and was fixed very precisely by statute in 1276 as 1 July 1189, the beginning of Richard I's reign. The idea was that if you could prove possession of land or a title or right from that date, there was no need to establish when or how it was originally acquired. Not surprisingly, everyone but the lawyers soon forgot the specific meaning and both phrases developed the more general sense of 'a very long time ago', as in 'People have been yearning for happy marriages since time immemorial.'

time is **money**

time is a valuable resource, so it's best to do things as quickly as possible

This expression has a very modern ring to it, in keeping with what we hear today about the 'money-rich but time-poor' lives of many in the West. In fact, the American statesman and scientist Benjamin Franklin seems to have coined it in 1748, in a speech entitled 'Advice to Young Tradesmen': 'Remember that time is money.' The thought has clearly impressed itself on the minds of many throughout the centuries, as the saying 'the most costly outlay is time' is attributed to the 5th-century BC Athenian orator and politician Antiphon.

tired and **emotional**

drunk

This euphemistic expression is particularly associated with the British satirical magazine *Private Eye*, and first appeared as *tired and overwrought* in September 1967 ('Mr Brown had been tired and overwrought on many occasions')—the reference was to the Labour MP and Cabinet minister George Brown. It was originally used to avoid describing someone in the public eye as being *drunk*, something which could potentially provoke a libel charge.

on your **tod**

alone

The source of this phrase is *on your Tod Sloan*, which is rhyming slang for 'on your own'. Tod Sloan was a famous American jockey who made his name in the 1890s, being immortalized in this expression some forty years later. An earlier parallel, used in Australia and New Zealand, is *on your pat*, which is short for *on your Pat Malone*: in this case, the name just seems to have been chosen for its familiarity and the rhyme, as no one has been able to trace a connection to a particular person.

tongue in **cheek**

speaking or writing in an ironic or insincere way

In former times, to *put your tongue in your cheek* meant 'speak insincerely'. This originated in a contemptuous gesture, common from at least the 18th century, which involved poking your tongue in your cheek. Rude gestures move on over time, and nowadays people tend to press their tongue under their lower lip as a mild display of derision or dislike: who knows, in a few years that might prompt a new phrase!

over the top
excessive or exaggerated

The expression *go over the top* originated in the First World War, when it was used to describe troops in the trenches charging over the parapets to attack the enemy. It gradually developed the meaning 'do something to an excessive or exaggerated degree', possibly in reference to the huge numbers of soldiers who died in the conflict. Soon the phrase was being shortened to simply *over the top*, and in modern use it has been reduced even further to the abbreviation *OTT*, as in 'The film that gave Halle Berry the chance to make one of the longest and most OTT Oscar acceptance speeches ever.'

a soft touch
someone who is easily manipulated

In the mid 19th century the word *touch* developed a number of slang meanings among the criminal fraternity. It described various ways of getting money from people, either by stealing, especially pickpocketing, or by some con trick, and soon also came to refer to the unfortunate person targeted in this way. A *soft touch* was someone who was particularly easy to con or steal from, and even today the phrase is often used to describe someone who is always willing to lend money to a friend.

over the transom
unsolicited

A *transom* is a crossbar set above a door or window, and the word is also used in American English for a small window above this crossbar. In long, hot days before the invention of air conditioning, office workers would leave these windows open to provide some token ventilation. Resourceful aspiring authors could take advantage of this and slip a manuscript through the open window to land on the office floor of some unsuspecting publishing editor. As a result, manuscripts delivered in this way were described as being *over the transom*, and the phrase was soon extended to anything offered or sent without prior agreement.

right as a *trivet*

in good health

A *trivet* is an iron tripod placed over a fire for a cooking pot or kettle to stand on. Its three legs make it very stable and so it came to be used in this expression as a symbol of soundness and steadiness. One of the earliest examples is found in *The Pickwick Papers* (1837) by Charles Dickens: '"I hope you are well, sir." "Right as a trivet, sir," replied Bob Sawyer.'

off your *trolley*

mad

The *trolley* in this expression has nothing to do with transporting patients round a hospital, nor does it refer to struggling round a local supermarket doing the weekly shop (though that could make you doubt your own or others' sanity sometimes). The *trolley* in question is in fact a pulley that runs along an overhead track and transmits power from the track to drive a tram. If a tram becomes disconnected from the pulley, it's no longer under control. A similar idea is found in *go off the rails* meaning 'begin behaving in an uncontrolled or unacceptable way', the image being of a train leaving the tracks or being derailed.

turn up *trumps*

produce a better performance or outcome than expected

The origins of this expression and the alternative *come up trumps* lie in card games. In bridge, whist, and similar games, *trumps* are cards of the suit that temporarily ranks above the other suits. In some forms the trump suit is chosen before each game (in bridge the right to choose is bid for); in others it is the suit of the last card dealt, which is turned over to show its face. This or a similar method is the one that gives rise to *turning* or *coming up trumps*. Of course, a hand with many trump cards is likely to be a winning hand. The word *trump* itself is actually an alteration of *triumph*, which was once used in card games in the same sense. The phrase featured in a headline to a 2004 article about the former wife of the American business magnate Donald Trump, 'Ivana Turns Up Trumps', referring to her own business success since her divorce.

in the *twinkling* of an eye

very quickly

Twinkling was used as an ordinary term for 'winking or blinking the eyes' from the 14th century right up until the early 19th century. The extended use meaning 'the time taken to wink or blink', i.e. 'a very short time', is just as old, but it probably survived in this expression because it appears in various passages in the Bible, most notably perhaps in Corinthians 15:51: 'In a moment, in the twinkling of an eye, at the last trump.' A similar expression containing the same idea is of course *in the blink of an eye*.

Uncle Tom Cobley and all
a whole lot of people

This expression is typically used as the last item in a long list of people, emphasizing that everyone possible has been included or considered, however inappropriately. It comes from an old song called 'Widdicombe Fair', dating from around 1800, which tells the tale of seven men all on one horse on their way to the fair at Widecombe-in-the-Moor in Devon: the song lists the men's names, ending with 'Uncle Tom Cobley and all'. The independent use of the phrase itself didn't develop until around a century later, in the 1930s.

on your uppers
very short of money

The *upper* is the part of a shoe above the sole, covering the top part of your foot. Worn-out shoes tend to be a sign of poverty, and if all someone has left of their shoes is the uppers, they are likely to be in a very impoverished state indeed.

the upper crust

the upper classes

The origins of this expression are the subject of some debate. One of the most popular explanations traces its roots back to medieval kitchens. The *crust* in question is the top part of a loaf of bread: it has been suggested that when a loaf was baked, the base, which was on the floor of the oven, tended to burn before the crust was properly browned. The upper crust would be cut off and reserved for the lords and ladies of the household, leaving the hard blackened remainder for the servants. Although the earliest literal example of the phrase does refer to 'cutting the upper crust for your sovereign', there are no examples of the phrase being used of the upper strata of society until the 1830s. It seems to have been a popular American term around that time, and also features in a glossary of Northamptonshire words and phrases published in 1854, where 'Mrs Upper Crust' is explained as the nickname for 'any female who assumes unauthorized superiority'. It seems likely that *crust* is simply being used in the sense of 'top layer': not nearly as good a story as the first suggestion!

variety is the spice of life

new and exciting experiences make life more interesting

We have the English poet William Cowper to thank for this familiar proverb. His poem 'The Task' (1785) contains the line: 'Variety's the very spice of life, That gives it all its flavour.' The dramatist Aphra Behn, who had a similar idea around a century earlier, might possibly have inspired him. Her version, from the play *The Rover* (1681), reads: 'Variety is the very soul of pleasure.'

beyond the veil

in a mysterious or hidden place or state

At first glance, this expression probably calls to mind the veil worn by some Muslim women to conceal their face from view. In fact it comes from a different meaning of *veil* altogether: in ancient times, the *veil* was the piece of precious cloth separating the innermost sanctuary from the rest of the Jewish Temple in Jerusalem. The idea soon developed of this cloth representing a barrier between this life and the unknown state of existence after death, giving rise to the current phrase.

on the wagon

abstaining from drinking alcohol

The original version of this expression was *on the water wagon*, which first appeared in America in the early 20th century. A *water wagon* was a sort of barrel on wheels, used to water dusty streets. These vehicles had been around since the early 18th century at least (in Britain they were known as *water carts*), but it may have been the increasing popularity of the temperance movement in the latter part of the 19th century and the idea of favouring water over wine or other alcohol that gave rise to the phrase. Of course, people can also come *off the wagon* and revert to their drinking ways, as this example from a 2003 edition of the magazine *Ice* illustrates: 'George Best has well and truly fallen off the wagon, lamping a News of the World photographer who spotted him boozing in a pub in Surrey.'

go walkabout

wander around from place to place in a leisurely way

In Australian English, a *walkabout* is a journey into the bush undertaken by an Aboriginal in order to live in a traditional way and re-establish contact with spiritual sources. The scope of the term was extended to describe a general wander about, and is often particularly used of the informal strolls among welcoming crowds favoured by members of the royal family and visiting dignitaries. These days the phrase is often used to mean 'go missing' or 'disappear', especially in the context of small objects such as pens, car keys, and television remote controls which have frustratingly vanished from your desk, bag, or sofa.

warts and all

including features or qualities that are not appealing or attractive

This expression dates back to the early 20th century, with the English writer Somerset Maugham taking credit for the earliest recorded example in his novel *Cakes and Ale* (1930): ' Don't you think it would be more interesting if you went the whole hog and drew him warts and all?' The source of the phrase can be traced back to Horace Walpole's *Anecdotes of Painting in England* (1763), in which he recounts a request supposedly made by Oliver Cromwell to the portrait painter Peter Lely: 'Remark all these roughnesses, pimples, warts, and everything as you see me; otherwise I will never pay a farthing for it.' Judging by other portraits of Cromwell, Lely was not alone in being given this brief!

the watches of the night

the hours of night, viewed as a time when you can't sleep

A *watch* was originally one of the periods of time into which the night was divided for the purposes of guard duty. Ancient Hebrew guards had the toughest job, as their night was only divided into three, whereas the Greeks and Romans had an easier time, with four or five watches and so a shorter spell on duty. The link with insomnia first appears in the writings of the Scottish novelist and poet Sir Walter Scott, who wrote in his journal for January 1826: 'The watches of the night pass wearily when disturbed by fruitless regrets.'

of the first water

unsurpassed of their kind, usually in a negative way

The word *water* has been used for centuries to describe the quality of brilliance or clarity of a diamond or pearl. The three highest grades into which stones could be classified used to be called *waters*, but only *first water*, the top one, is found today, describing a completely flawless gem. An equivalent term is found in many European languages, and all are thought to come from the Arabic word for water, which also meant 'shine or splendour', presumably from the appearance of very pure water. People and things other than gems began to be described as *of the first water* in the 1820s, but the phrase quite quickly acquired its current, rather negative associations. Nowadays it is very rarely a compliment to be described as 'something of the first water'. In a letter written in 1950, P. G. Wodehouse commented disparagingly on J. M. Barrie's play *The Admirable Crichton*: 'I remember being entranced with it in 1904 or whenever it was, but now it seems like a turkey of the first water.'

go west

be killed or meet with some other disaster

The image behind this expression is of the sun setting in the west at the end of the day. The meaning 'die or be killed' became common during the First World War; quite why is not clear. The expression is also used more generally in the sense 'be lost or broken', and this is the meaning found in the recent American equivalent *go south*. The choice of a different compass point is possibly connected with the idea of something being on a downward trend, or perhaps *go west* sounded too positive, given the hopeful promise of the American West represented in the well-known exhortation 'Go west, young man! Go west!'

a wet blanket

someone who spoils other people's fun with their disapproving manner

Miserable party-poopers have doubtless been around since the dawn of humankind, but the idea of comparing them to a wet blanket doesn't seem to have arisen until the 1850s. The reference is to the use of a dampened blanket to smother a fire, the image being of a gloomy or disapproving person subduing or casting a damper on the lively, cheerful mood of others.

blow the whistle on someone

bring an illicit activity to an end by informing on the person responsible

This expression, which dates back to the 1930s, has a sporting background. In football and other sports, the referee will blow a whistle to indicate that a player has broken the rules and that play must be temporarily stopped. When the expression was first used in other contexts it simply meant 'bring an activity to an abrupt halt', but by the 1970s the current meaning had taken over. It has spawned a number of related terms, such as *whistle-blower* and *whistle-blowing*.

a white elephant

a useless or unwanted possession, especially one that's expensive to maintain

For centuries the rare albino elephant was regarded as holy in some Asian countries. It was especially prized by the kings of Siam (present-day Thailand) and its upkeep was extremely expensive. The story goes that it was the custom for a king of Siam to give one of these elephants to a courtier he particularly disliked: the unfortunate recipient could neither refuse the gift nor give it away later for fear of causing offence, and would end up financially ruined by the costs of looking after the animal. New public buildings are popular candidates for the title of *white elephant*, as in this example from an article in *The Times* comparing the new Scottish Parliament Building and the Millennium Dome, both projects which went wildly over budget: 'At least Scotland got a masterpiece instead of a white elephant.'

wild and woolly

uncouth in appearance or behaviour

This expression was originally applied to the western United States in the 19th century, when it was a lawless frontier popularly also known as the Wild West, of course. The *woolly* part of the phrase probably arose from the typical clothing worn by the pioneers and cowboys of the area, who favoured the natural look of jerkins made of sheepskin with the wool still attached. The phrase is often used to refer to a general disregard for rules, as illustrated by this example from a report in the *Sydney Morning Herald* on a forthcoming rugby tour: 'The squad . . . will play four matches in 14 days, with the coaching staff and players expecting a wild and woolly time in South America.'

a *wild* goose chase

a foolish and hopeless search for something unattainable

The origin of this expression is not quite as clear-cut as it might appear. The obvious suggestion is that it alludes to the difficulty of shooting wild geese flying very fast and high in the sky. However, early examples, dating from the late 16th century, refer to a popular sport of the time in which each of a line of riders had to follow accurately the course of the leader, like a flight of wild geese.

sail close to the wind

verge on indecency, dishonesty, or disaster

To sail in the direction the wind is blowing from, a boat has to zigzag across it. You want to sail as close to directly into the wind as you can, but if you get too close the sail starts to flap, the boat slows down, and, as the wind gets on the wrong side of the sail, you start to go backwards. Disaster can strike in two ways: either the force of the wind will bring the mast down, or, if you're trying to sail away from the shore and start going backwards, you could be wrecked on the rocks.

in the *wings*

ready to do something or to be used at the appropriate time

The origins of this expression lie in the world of the theatre. The *wings* are the sides of the stage screened from the audience, where actors wait for their cue to come on stage: the longer version *wait in the wings* conveys this image even more clearly. The phrase is often used in sporting or political contexts to refer to someone ready to take a leading role, as in this example from Nesta Wyn Ellis's biography of the Conservative prime minister John Major: 'Michael Heseltine was always the understudy waiting in the wings to be the star of the show.'

on a *wing* and a prayer

with only the slightest chance of success

This expression comes from the title of a 1943 song by the American songwriter Harold Adamson, 'Comin' in on a Wing and a Pray'r'. He himself took it from a comment made by a wartime pilot speaking to ground control just before he made an emergency landing in his damaged plane.

wing it

do something without preparation

Like *in the wings*, this expression comes from the theatre. Actors used to talk about 'winging a part', meaning that they had to play a role before they knew their lines properly, either studying the part in the wings in between their scenes or relying on someone prompting them from the wings when they forgot their words. *Wing it* was used in this sense from the late 19th century, but didn't acquire its more general meaning of 'improvise' until the 1950s. In one of his diaries (which were published in 1982), the English actor and dramatist Noel Coward remarked: 'I decided to use irrepressible laughter as the basis of my performance and just wing it on that one technical trick.'

wipe the slate clean

make a fresh start

In the past, shopkeepers and pub landlords used to keep a record of what a customer owed them by writing the details on a slate tablet. Once the customer had paid their account, the slate would literally be wiped clean. Slates have been used in this way at least since medieval times, but it wasn't until the late 19th century that someone had the idea of comparing cleaning a slate to forgetting about past disagreements.

down to the wire

used to describe a situation whose outcome isn't decided until the very last minute

This expression originated in North America and comes from the world of horse racing. Racecourses there have a wire stretched across and above the finishing line: a race that goes *down to the wire* is one in which the horses are neck and neck right to the finish. The phrase is now used of any close contest or tense, undecided situation, from the battle to be top of the Premiership in football to the next US presidential election: 'The championship could go right down to the wire with Manchester United having to face Liverpool, Newcastle, and Arsenal in their next three games.'

witching hour

midnight

The popular superstition that witches and other ghouls and ghosts are at their most active in the middle of the night was exploited by Shakespeare in *Hamlet*.

Hamlet himself declares: 'Tis now the very witching time of night, When churchyards yawn, and hell itself breathes out contagion to this world.' Over the centuries many have followed Shakespeare's example, including the American writer Washington Irving (1783–1859) in his chilling tale 'The Legend of Sleepy Hollow': 'As he wended his way, by swamp and stream and awful woodland . . . every sound of nature, at that witching hour, fluttered his excited imagination.'

cry wolf

call for help when it isn't needed

This expression goes back to the tale of the shepherd boy and the wolf, one of the famous fables of Aesop, a Greek storyteller of the 6th century BC. In the story, a shepherd boy guarding a flock of sheep kept summoning the local villagers with cries of 'Wolf! Wolf!'. Each time the villagers rushed to help, he would laugh and say he was only joking, until eventually they no longer took any notice of him. When one day a wolf did appear and attack him, his (this time genuine) cries for help were ignored and no one came to save him.

a wolf in sheep's clothing

a person who appears friendly but is in fact hostile or dangerous

It was Jesus who first referred to this type of person, in the Sermon on the Mount, as recounted in the Gospel of St Matthew (7:15): 'Beware of false prophets, which come to you in sheep's clothing, but inwardly they are ravening wolves.' The contrast is of course between the docile domesticated creature and the ferocious wild animal: in a famous exploitation of the phrase, the Conservative leader Winston Churchill once dismissed his Labour opposite number Clement Attlee as 'a sheep in sheep's clothing'.

throw someone to the wolves

leave someone to be harshly treated without trying to help them

This expression is surprisingly recent, being recorded only from the 1920s. A popular explanation for its origins links it to tales about packs of wolves pursuing travellers in horse-drawn sleighs: one unfortunate person would be pushed off the sleigh to lessen the load and allow the sleigh to go faster, so enabling the others to make their escape.

spin a yarn
tell a long, far-fetched story

This expression is nautical in origin. An important job on board ship was making and repairing ropes, a task which involved twisting together a number of long threads or *yarns*. The image of this process and the reputation sailors had for telling tall tales of fabulous far-flung lands combined to produce the phrase we know today.

Thematic index

This section contains groups of phrases which are linked by a common theme or subject. The themes are listed in alphabetical order and the word in **bold** print indicates where individual phrases are to be found in the main book, or, where there is a cross-reference to a panel, gives guidance as to the section of the panel containing the phrase.

Action

jump on the **bandwagon**
beat about the bush
a **ginger** group
heave in sight
hit the ground running
by **hook** or by crook
have many **irons** in the fire
knock something on the head
rest on your **laurels**
enter the **lists**
pull the plug
from **scratch**
lick someone *or* something into **shape**
surf the net
wipe the slate clean

Age

have had a good **innings**
long in the tooth
mutton dressed as lamb: see EATING
    AND DRINKING panel
your **salad** days

Ambition

push the **envelope**
room at the top
in your **sights**

Anger and annoyance

go **ape**
get somone's **back** up
make your blood boil (*at* make your
    blood run cold)
effing and blinding
at the **end** of your tether
give someone the hairy **eyeball**
light the blue touchpaper
give someone the **pip**
a **red** rag to a bull: see COLOURS panel
see **red**: see COLOURS panel
let off **steam**

Anxiety and fear

get the **all-clear**
with **bated** breath
make your **blood** run cold *or* curdle
lay a ghost
scare the living daylights out of (*at* beat
    the living **daylights** out of)
on **tenterhooks**

Appearance

as **bald** as a coot
bells and whistles
borrowed plumes
fine feathers make fine birds (*at*
    borrowed plumes)

the **cut** of someone's jib
a **false** dawn
as large as **life**
a **motley** crew
mutton dressed as lamb: see EATING
    AND DRINKING panel
ragtag and bobtail
shades of —
be the **spit** of
warts and all
wild and woolly
a **wolf** in sheep's clothing

Argument and conflict

up the **ante**
call someone's **bluff**
fight like **cat** and dog: see ANIMALS
    panel
play **devil**'s advocate
no **holds** barred
an **honest** broker
at **loggerheads**
a **pitched** battle
pour oil on troubled waters
run high
a **running** battle

Certainty

the **acid** test
true **blue**: see COLOURS panel
on the **cards**
by a long **chalk**
the **die** is cast
straight from the **horse**'s mouth
the real **McCoy**
not on your **nelly**
a **smoking** gun

Change

chop and change
die hard

dyed in the wool
against the **grain**
stick to your **guns**
Jekyll and Hyde
turn over a new **leaf**
break the **mould**
rise from the ashes: see LEGENDS AND
    MYTHS panel
in a **rut**
be set in **stone**
turn the **tables**
variety is the spice of life

Chaos and disorder

a **dog's** dinner or breakfast: see
    ANIMALS panel
let the **genie** out of the bottle
out of **hand**: see PARTS OF THE BODY
    panel
far from the **madding** crowd
that way **madness** lies
Pandora's box
shipshape and Bristol fashion
at **sixes** and sevens
a **tangled** web

Class

blue blood: see COLOURS panel
pull yourself up by your (own)
    bootstraps
keep up with the **Joneses**
born to the **purple**
sit below the **salt**
the **upper** crust

Cooperation and help

aid and **abet**
under the **auspices** of
turn a **blind** eye
in **cahoots**
a **good** Samaritan: see BIBLICAL panel

kick over the traces
if the **mountain** won't come to
    Muhammad, Muhammad must go
    to the mountain
in **tandem**

Courage

bite the bullet
have a lot of **bottle**
with your **eyes** open: see PARTS OF THE
    BODY panel
run the **gauntlet**
throw down *or* take up the **gauntlet**
gird up your loins
grasp the nettle
a **heart** of oak
out on a **limb**
enter the **lists**
put someone on their **mettle**
stiff upper lip

Crime and punishment

on the **carpet**
haul someone over the **coals**
send someone to **Coventry**
the **devil** to pay
take the **fall**
be for the **high** jump
off the **hook**
no **names**, no pack drill
take the **rap**
read the riot act
caught **red**-handed: see COLOURS panel

Crisis

burn your boats *or* bridges
cross the Rubicon
at the **eleventh** hour: see BIBLICAL
    panel
fiddle while Rome burns
the tip of the **iceberg**

the bottom **line**
the **moment** of truth
paper over the cracks
the last *or* final **straw**

Critics and criticism

below the **belt**
be in someone's **black** books
a **flea** in your ear
don't look a **gift** horse in the mouth
blow a **raspberry**

Danger

a shot across the **bows**
chance your arm
dice with death
go through **fire** and water
a **hostage** to fortune
a **loose** cannon
saved by the bell: see SPORT panel
a **siren** call: see LEGENDS AND MYTHS
    panel
sword of Damocles
sail close to the **wind**

Death

go to **Davy Jones's locker**
dead as a **doornail**
give up the **ghost**
kick the bucket
shuffle off this mortal coil: see
    SHAKESPEARE panel
beyond the **veil**
go **west**

Debt

in **hock**
your **pound** of flesh
call it **quits**
in the **red**: see COLOURS panel

rob Peter to pay Paul
on **tick**

Deception and dishonesty

in **cahoots**
show your true **colours**
cook the books
economical with the truth
play **fast** and loose
beware of **Greeks** bearing gifts: see
    LEGENDS AND MYTHS panel
hook, line, and sinker
swing the lead: see NAUTICAL panel
tongue in cheek
cry **wolf**
spin a **yarn**

Doubt and uncertainty

a **doubting** Thomas: see BIBLICAL panel
a **grey** area
on the **horns** of a dilemma
a **joker** in the pack
tell that to the **marines**
no man's land
the **plot** thickens
down to the **wire**

Drinking

Dutch courage: see FOREIGN
    COUNTRIES panel
one over the **eight**
hair of the dog
three **sheets** to the wind: see NAUTICAL
    panel
spit and sawdust
the **sun** is over the yardarm
as **tight** as a tick
tired and emotional
on the **wagon**

Drugs

chase the dragon
go **cold** turkey
slip someone a **Mickey Finn**

Duty and responsibility

step into the **breach**
pass the **buck**
lay something at someone's **door**
be someone's **pigeon**
cock a **snook**
toe the line: see SPORT panel
wash your hands of: see BIBLICAL panel

Equality

across the board
an **even** break
play second **fiddle**
neck and neck: see SPORT panel
ours not to **reason** why
all roads lead to **Rome**: see FOREIGN
    COUNTRIES panel
separate the **sheep** from the goats

Excess and extravagance

kill the **fatted** calf: see BIBLICAL panel
jump the shark
go **overboard**
over-egg the pudding
a **prodigal** son: see BIBLICAL panel
put on the **ritz**
over the **top**

Expense

an **arm** and a leg
not worth the **candle**
go **Dutch**: see FOREIGN COUNTRIES
    panel
a **king**'s ransom

for a **song**
time is money
a **white** elephant

Failure

go by the **board**: see NAUTICAL panel
a **damp** squib
dead as a dodo
a **dead** cat bounce
a **false** start: see SPORT panel
Hamlet without the prince
the **kiss** of death
Murphy's law
go **phut**
make a **pig's** ear of: see ANIMALS panel
win the wooden **spoon**
throw in the towel
thumbs down (*at* **thumbs** up)
go **west**

Fate and chance

fall *or* land on your feet
finders keepers
speak *or* talk of the **devil**
in the **lap** of the gods
someone's **number** is up
on a **wing** and a prayer

Foresight and the future

cross someone's palm with silver
in the **offing**
a **pricking** in your thumbs
a **rainy** day

Forgiveness and reconciliation

bury the hatchet
a sop to **Cerberus**: see LEGENDS AND
    MYTHS panel
hold out an **olive** branch

a **prodigal** son: see BIBLICAL panel
turn the other cheek: see BIBLICAL
    panel

Futility

build **castles** in the air
kick against the pricks
never-never land
paint the Forth Bridge
pie in the sky
from **pillar** to post
a **Pyrrhic** victory
a **wild** goose chase

Gossip and rumour

your **ears** are burning
bush **telegraph**

Happiness, pleasure, and enjoyment

full of **beans**
beer and skittles: see EATING AND
    DRINKING panel
bread and circuses
go a **bundle** on
the **cherry** on the cake: see EATING AND
    DRINKING panel
on **cloud** nine
happy as a sandboy *or* a clam
happy hunting ground
to your **heart's** content: see
    SHAKESPEARE panel
high days and holidays
over the **moon**
in **stitches**
on the **tiles**
days of **wine** and roses: see EATING AND
    DRINKING panel
wine, women, and song: see EATING
    AND DRINKING panel

Haste and speed

like the **clappers**
like the deuce (*at* the **deuce** of a —)
like a **dose** of salts
at a rate of **knots**
be quick *or* slow off the **mark**: see SPORT
    panel
in the **twinkling** of an eye

Health and illness

a clean **bill** of health
in fine **fettle**
in the **pink**
as sick as a dog (*at* as **sick** as a parrot)
as right as a **trivet**

Intelligence and knowledge

in a **brown** study
double **Dutch**: see FOREIGN COUNTRIES
    panel
it's all **Greek** to me: see FOREIGN
    COUNTRIES panel
use your **loaf**
be quick *or* slow off the **mark**: see SPORT
    panel
no news is good news
a **nod**'s as good as a wink
a **nose** for: see PARTS OF THE BODY panel
know your **onions**
the **penny** has dropped
plain as a pikestaff
rack your brains
have someone *or* something **taped**

Jealousy and envy

a **chip** on your shoulder
keep up with the **Joneses**
sour grapes

Laziness and sleep

couch potato
dog tired: see ANIMALS panel
forty winks
the **land** of Nod
swing the lead: see NAUTICAL panel

Madness

mad as a hatter *or* a March hare
go **postal**
off your **trolley**
go off the rails (*at* off your **trolley**)

Misfortune

go for a **Burton**
cook someone's goose
come a **cropper**
the **deuce** of a —
a **dog's** life: see ANIMALS panel
grin and bear it
a pretty *or* fine **kettle** of fish
a **millstone** round your neck
go **pear-shaped**
go to **pot**
hit the **skids**
slings and arrows: see SHAKESPEARE
    panel

Mistakes

back to square one
drop a clanger
kill the **goose** that lays the golden egg
make a **hash** of

Money

in the **black**: see COLOURS panel
have your **bread** buttered on both sides:
    see EATING AND DRINKING panel
make money **hand** over fist

the Old **Lady** of Threadneedle Street
the **Midas** touch
on the **nail**
when someone's **ship** comes in
a **white** knight: see COLOURS panel

Nakedness

in the **buff**
go **commando**

Opportunity

within an **ace** of
strike while the **iron** is hot
open sesame
opportunity knocks
in **pole** position
room at the top
have many **strings** to your bow
time and tide wait for no man
over the **transom**

Poverty

on your **beam** ends: see NAUTICAL panel
down and out: see SPORT panel
on your **uppers**

Power

hold all the **aces**
have someone over a **barrel**
be at someone's **beck** and call
a **big** cheese
hold all the **cards**
play **cat** and mouse with: see ANIMAL
    panel
a **firm** hand
a free **hand**: see PARTS OF THE BODY
    panel
have your **hands** tied: see PARTS OF THE
    BODY panel
give someone their **head**

pull strings
rule with a **rod** of iron: see BIBLICAL
    panel
rule the roost

Preparation and readiness

clear the decks
off the **cuff**
gird up your loins
jump the **gun**: see SPORT panel
at **half** cock
on the **qui vive**
in the **wings**
wing it

Quality and excellence

A1
the **bee**'s knees: see ANIMALS panel
cannot hold a **candle** to
the **cat**'s whiskers: see ANIMALS panel
credit where credit is due: see BIBLICAL
    panel
a **curate**'s egg
go the **distance**
the **dog**'s bollocks: see ANIMALS panel
of the **first** magnitude
the **flower** of —
with **flying** colours
in the **groove**
a dab **hand**: see PARTS OF THE BODY
    panel
knock spots off
be **mentioned** in dispatches
be the **pits**
pure as the driven snow
a **rough** diamond
run of the mill
the **salt** of the earth: see EATING AND
    DRINKING panel
worth your **salt**: see EATING AND
    DRINKING panel
sweet spot

to a **T** *or* tee
of the first **water**

Reputation and fame

a **black** sheep: see COLOURS panel
not as **black** as you are painted: see
    COLOURS panel
Caesar's wife
a name to **conjure** with
beyond the **pale**
come up **smelling** of roses
whiter than **white**: see COLOURS panel

Secrecy

have an **ace** up your sleeve
keep your cards close to your chest (*at*
    hold all the **cards**)
in (*or* out of) the **closet**
a **dark** horse
mum's the word
smoke-filled **rooms**
behind the **scenes**
blow the **whistle** on someone
have a **word** in someone's ear: see
    SHAKESPEARE panel

Self-Interest

save your **bacon**: see EATING AND
    DRINKING panel
beat a hasty retreat
know which side your **bread** is buttered
    on: see EATING AND DRINKING panel
curry favour
cut and run
dog eat dog: see ANIMALS panel
have an **eye** for the main chance
give your **eye teeth** for
not care *or* give a **fig**
be **hoist** with your own petard: see
    SHAKESPEARE panel

not in my back yard
sell your soul
stake a claim
steal someone's thunder
throw someone to the **wolves**

Success

bring home the **bacon**: see EATING AND
    DRINKING panel
blaze a trail
Bob's your uncle
close but no **cigar**
break your **duck**
fall *or* land on your feet
a **feather** in your cap
a **flash** in the pan
flavour of the month
hands down: see SPORT panel
happy hunting ground
hit the **jackpot**
no **pain**, no gain
square the circle
turn up **trumps**
thumbs up

Surprise

be taken **aback**: see NAUTICAL panel
out of the **blue**
your **eyes** are out on stalks: see PARTS
    OF THE BODY panel
knock someone for **six**

Thoroughness

all-singing, all-dancing
to **boot**
by and large
the whole (kit and) **caboodle**
at one **fell** swoop: see SHAKESPEARE
    panel
run the **gamut**

go the whole **hog**
lock, stock, and barrel
go the extra **mile**: see BIBLICAL panel
the full **monty**
part and parcel of
pull out all the **stops**
Uncle Tom Cobley and all

Time

crack of dawn
for **donkey**'s years: see ANIMALS panel
early doors
a movable **feast**
long time no see
a **month** of Sundays
time immemorial *or* **time** out of mind
the **watches** of the night
the **witching** hour

Traitors and treachery

fifth column
beware of **Greeks** bearing gifts: see
    LEGENDS AND MYTHS panel
a **Judas** kiss: see BIBLICAL panel
night of the long knives
sell someone down the **river**
a **snake** in the grass
spike someone's guns
put a **spoke** in someone's wheel
a **Trojan** horse: see LEGENDS AND MYTHS
    panel

Unhappiness and disappointment

turn to **ashes** in your mouth
have the **blues**: see COLOURS panel

a **damp** squib
a **dog**'s life: see ANIMALS panel
a ghost *or* spectre at the **feast**
a **Job**'s comforter: see BIBLICAL panel
down in the **mouth**: see PARTS OF THE
    BODY panel
keep your **pecker** up
cut someone to the **quick**
as **sick** as a parrot
a **wet** blanket

Weakness

an **Achilles** heel: see LEGENDS AND
    MYTHS panel
feet of clay
a soft **touch**

Weather

brass monkey
rain cats and dogs

Work and employment

a **baker**'s dozen
someone's **bread** and butter: see
    EATING AND DRINKING panel
take the **bread** out of people's mouths:
    see EATING AND DRINKING panel
the **ghost** walks
a **man** of the cloth
show someone the **ropes**
get your **teeth** into something: see
    PARTS OF THE BODY panel
make heavy **weather** of: see NAUTICAL
    panel

WITHDRAWN

DANVILLE PUBLIC LIBRARY

32604020133249

$2 Fine For Removing
the Bar Code Label

WITHDRAWN

T 133249

DANVILLE PUBLIC LIBRARY
DANVILLE, INDIANA